Get by in BUSINESS GERMAN

A QUICK BEGINNER'S COURSE FOR BUSINESS PEOPLE

● REINHARD TENBERG ●

BBC BOOKS

Published by BBC Books
a division of BBC Enterprises Ltd
Woodlands, 80 Wood Lane
London W12 0TT

First published 1993

© Reinhard Tenberg 1993
The moral right of the author has been asserted

ISBN 0 563 36418 1

Designed by Gwyn Lewis
Maps and illustrations by Julian Bingley
Cover design by Paul Oldman
Cover illustration by Nick Sharratt

Photo credits: pages 17 and 22 Monika Müller;
pages 28 and 38 Image Bank;
page 96 Anthony Blake Photo Library

Audio cassettes produced by
Colette Thomson, Footsteps Productions Ltd

Set in Great Britain by
Goodfellow & Egan Phototypesetting Ltd, Cambridge
Printed and bound in Great Britain by Clays Ltd, St Ives Plc
Cover printed by Clays Ltd, St Ives Plc

Exclusive U.S. Distributor of the Get By In Series Packs
Ambrose Video Publishing Inc.
1290 Avenue of the Americas
Suite 2245, New York, N.Y. 10104

CONTENTS

Introduction — 5

Map — 9

UNIT 1 **Getting there** — 10
At the airport
Using public transport

UNIT 2 **Introductions** — 24
Making an appointment
Telephone appointments
Cancelling an appointment
Face-to-face introductions

UNIT 3 **Enquiries** — 41
Making contact
Asking for a catalogue
Enquiring about the stock situation
Delivery time and discount
The first order

UNIT 4 **Business problems** — 58
Making a complaint
Dealing with a complaint
Delivery problems
An overdue payment

UNIT 5	Coping with correspondence	**74**
	Acknowledgement of order	
	An unsuccessful booking	
	Hotel reservation	
	Querying an invoice	
	Production problems	
	Cancellation of an order	
UNIT 6	Wining and dining	**94**
	An invitation	
	At the restaurant	
	Thank you and goodbye	

Reference section	107
Key to exercises	110
Word list	116

INTRODUCTION

THE RIGHT COURSE FOR ME?

Get by in Business German is a six-unit course for anyone doing business with or in a German-speaking country. If you have little or no knowledge of German and wish to progress quickly, this course is for you. It consists of two audiocassettes as well as this book.

Get by in Business German will not turn you into a fluent German speaker within three weeks. Nothing can, despite the claims of some advertisements to the contrary. But the course will help you to:

- Make yourself understood in some basic business situations, such as finding your way around on a business trip, introducing yourself and your company, making an appointment on the telephone, and so on
- Understand what people say to you
- Get to grips with simple business correspondence
- Make a few friends and get more out of your business trips by 'having a go' at the language.

THE BOOK

Each of the six units in the book includes:

- Complete lists of key words and phrases
- Transcripts of the recorded dialogues
- Brief explanations of language points, with examples
- Exercises to help you to practise your skills

- Useful tips and brief notes on German business culture
- A self-assessment guide to monitor your progress.

At the back of the book, you'll find a reference section containing a simple guide to German pronunciation (you can listen to this at the beginning of the second cassette) and some useful language notes. There is also a key to the exercises and a German–English word list in alphabetical order.

THE AUDIOCASSETTES

The cassettes:

- Introduce the language you need to speak and understand in each situation
- Contain all dialogues reproduced in this book
- Include some tape-only dialogues to test your understanding in real business situations
- Give you plenty of opportunity to repeat words and expressions aloud, answer simple questions and take part in conversations similar to those you may encounter when using your German at work
- Allow you to study at your own pace.

TO MAKE THE MOST OF THE COURSE

- Firstly, look through the relevant unit in the book to give yourself an idea of what to expect.
- Start by listening to the tape. Listen to each unit section by section. You will recognize the start of a new section by a jingle that corresponds to the tape symbol in your book.
- Stop the tape after each section, go back to the book, study the word list and read the dialogue transcripts again. If you are unsure about the pronunciation, rewind the tape and listen again.

- Before listening to the next section, study the explanations and try the exercises.
- At the end of each unit, check your answers against the key at the back of the book, read the 'Worth Knowing' section and complete the self-assessment guide.
- When listening to the cassette, always join in aloud and, if you don't get the exercise quite right the first time, rewind the cassette and listen again. If a pause isn't long enough, use the pause button on your cassette player to extend it. Go through the exercises several times until you can do them without making mistakes.
- One final suggestion: if you're learning with someone else, take advantage of the opportunity to 'act out' the dialogues. You'll soon be able to remember them without your book.

Viel Spaß und guten Erfolg im Geschäft!

THE LÄNDER (STATES) OF THE FEDERAL REPUBLIC OF GERMANY

Bundesland	Area (sq. metres)	Population (in 1,000)	Industry (main branches)
Baden-Württemberg	35,751	9,619	Motor vehicles; electrical engineering
Bayern	70,553	11,221	Motor vehicles; mechanical engineering
Berlin	883	3,410	Pharmaceuticals; tourism; administration
Brandenburg	29,059	2,641	Food; mechanical engineering; textiles
Bremen	404	674	Transport
Hamburg	755	1,626	Petroleum products; food
Hessen	21,114	5,661	Chemicals; precious metals motor vehicles; banking
Mecklenburg-Vorpommern	23,838	1,964	Food; pharmaceuticals; shipbuilding
Niedersachsen	47,439	7,284	Motor vehicles; metals; energy
Nordrhein-Westfalen	34,068	17,104	Energy; chemicals; petroleum products; steel; coal mining
Rheinland-Pfalz	19,848	3,702	Chemicals
Saarland	2,569	1,065	Energy; coal mining
Sachsen	18,337	4,901	Motor vehicles; machinery textiles
Sachsen-Anhalt	20,445	2,965	Mechanical engineering; Chemicals
Schleswig-Holstein	15,728	2,595	Shipbuilding; chemicals
Thüringen	16,251	2,684	Electrical engineering; instrument engineering

Figures from *Statistisches Jahrbuch*, 1990; *Wirtschaft und Statistik*, 2/1991; Statistisches Amt der DDR, *Statistische Daten 1989 über die Länder der DDR*.

GETTING THERE

● STARTING OUT ●

Start each lesson by listening to the first set of dialogues, exercises and explanations on tape. Then look at the key words and phrases in your book. Read them aloud and use the tape to check your pronunciation. There is, of course, a complete list of words and phrases at the end of the book. You should then follow the explanations and complete the exercises in your book before returning to the next set of dialogues on tape.

● AT THE AIRPORT ●

KEY WORDS AND PHRASES	
entschuldigen Sie bitte	excuse me please
Entschuldigung	excuse me
wo ist . . . ?	where is . . . ?
der nächste Taxistand	the nearest taxi rank
vor dem Hauptausgang	in front of the main exit
danke schön/vielen Dank	thank you/many thanks
bitte/bitte schön	you're welcome
gibt es . . . ?	is there . . . ?
die Bank (-en)	bank
das Restaurant (-s)	restaurant
der Kiosk (-e)	kiosk

wie komme ich zur/zum . . . ?	how do I get to . . . ?
die Messe (-n)	trade fair
die Buchmesse (-n)	book fair
die S-Bahn (-en)	fast city train
der Bahnhof (¨e)	station
der Hauptbahnhof (¨e)	main station
die Straßenbahn (-en)	tram
die Linie 16 oder 19	number 16 or 19 (tram or bus)
ist das weit?	is that far?
etwa 40 Minuten mit der Bahn	about 40 minutes by train

At the airport

1.1 WHERE IS . . . ?

HERR WINKLER Entschuldigen Sie bitte, wo ist der nächste Taxistand?
ANGESTELLTE Vor dem Hauptausgang rechts.
HERR WINKLER Danke schön.
ANGESTELLTE Bitte.

1.2 IS THERE . . . NEARBY?

HERR WINKLER Entschuldigen Sie bitte, gibt es hier eine Bank in der Nähe?
PASSANT Ja, gehen Sie geradeaus, dann an dem Restaurant links, die Bank ist neben dem Kiosk.
HERR WINKLER Vielen Dank.

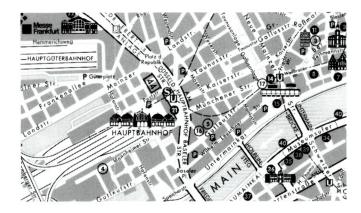

1.3 HOW DO I GET TO...?

HERR WINKLER	Entschuldigen Sie bitte, wie komme ich zur Frankfurter Buchmesse?
ANGESTELLTE	Nehmen Sie die S-Bahn zum Hauptbahnhof und dann die Straßenbahn, Linie 16 oder 19 zur Messe.
HERR WINKLER	Ist das weit?
ANGESTELLTE	Etwa 40 Minuten mit der Bahn.
HERR WINKLER	Vielen Dank!
ANGESTELLTE	Bitte schön.

EXPLANATIONS AND EXERCISES

'The' and 'a'

There are three noun genders in German: masculine, feminine and neuter (marked m., f. and n. in dictionaries), which you need to learn with the noun. The words you use for 'the' and 'a' vary accordingly.

	Masculine	Feminine	Neuter
the	**der** Bahnhof	**die** Messe	**das** Taxi
a/an	**ein** Bahnhof	**eine** Messe	**ein** Taxi

Numbers 0–100

Numbers are crucial for 'getting by' in business. You need them to cope with prices, phone numbers, invoices, etc. You'll find them in the pronunciation guide at the beginning of the second tape.

0 *null*	10 *zehn*	20 *zwanzig*	30 *dreißig*
1 *eins*	11 *elf*	21 *einundzwanzig*	31 *einunddreißig*
2 *zwei*	12 *zwölf*	22 *zweiundzwanzig*	40 *vierzig*
3 *drei*	13 *dreizehn*	23 *dreiundzwanzig*	50 *fünfzig*
4 *vier*	14 *vierzehn*	24 *vierundzwanzig*	60 *sechzig*
5 *fünf*	15 *fünfzehn*	25 *fünfundzwanzig*	70 *siebzig*
6 *sechs*	16 *sechzehn*	26 *sechsundzwanzig*	80 *achtzig*
7 *sieben*	17 *siebzehn*	27 *siebenundzwanzig*	90 *neunzig*
8 *acht*	18 *achtzehn*	28 *achtundzwanzig*	100 *einhundert*
9 *neun*	19 *neunzehn*	29 *neunundzwanzig*	(or. *hundert*)

Have you worked out the rule? Suppose you need to say 32 in German. Quite literally you say 'two and thirty' or *zweiunddreißig*.

EXERCISE 1.1
Write down the following numbers in German:

a 35
b 41
c 59
d 88
e 96

Asking directions
Start by saying *Entschuldigen Sie bitte, . . .* or *Entschuldigung, . . .* then simply add *wo ist . . .* followed by the place you are looking for:

Entschuldigen Sie bitte, wo ist der Bahnhof?
Entschuldigung, wo ist das Restaurant Melle?

EXERCISE 1.2
Ask where the following places are:

a Firma Häussler
b Hauptausgang
c Hotel zum goldenen Löwen

Someone might answer your last question by saying 'it's in the Lindenstraße'. You will then have to ask how to get there:

Wie komme ich . . .
- *zum Bahnhof?* (m.)
- *zum Restaurant?* (n.)
- *zur Lindenstraße?* (f.)
- *nach Frankfurt?*

When asking directions you use *zum* (*zu dem*) with masculine and neuter nouns and *zur* (*zu der*) with feminine nouns. With names of towns and most countries you use *nach*.

EXERCISE 1.3
Ask for directions to the following places:

a the main station
b the *S-Bahn*
c the trade fair
d Frankfurt

GIVING DIRECTIONS

rechts	right/on the right
links	left/on the left
vor dem/der	in front of the
neben dem/der	next to the
gegenüber dem/der	opposite the
in der Nähe	near/nearby
da drüben	over there
gleich hier vorne	just here
die nächste Straße	the next street
nehmen Sie die erste links	take the first on the left

gehen Sie geradeaus	go straight on
auf der linken/rechten Seite	on the left-hand/right-hand side
zum/zur	to the
bis zum/zur	up to/as far as the
bis zur nächsten Kreuzung	up to/as far as the next crossroads

Note that in directions using *vor*, *neben* or *gegenüber*, 'the' becomes *dem* with masculine and neuter nouns and *der* with feminine nouns:

*Der Bahnhof ist neben **dem** Kiosk. (der Kiosk)*
*Das Hotel ist gegenüber **dem** Restaurant. (das Restaurant)*
*Der Taxistand ist gegenüber **der** Firma. (die Firma)*

EXERCISE 1.4
Give the following directions in German:

Go straight on, then take the next on the right, go up to Lindenstraße. The hotel is opposite the station.

● USING PUBLIC TRANSPORT ●

KEY WORDS AND PHRASES

abfahren	to leave from
wo fährt die Straßenbahn ab?	where does the tram leave from?
die Haltestelle (-n)	bus or tram stop
zwei Minuten zu Fuß	two minutes' walk
ich möchte zur Messe	I'd like to go to the trade fair
welche Zone ist das?	which zone is it?
Moment bitte	just a moment
einmal nach . . ., bitte	a ticket to . . ., please
einfach/hin und zurück	single/return
erster/zweiter Klasse?	first/second class?
wieviel kostet das?	how much is that?
das macht . . . DM	that'll be . . . DM
DM = Deutsche Mark	German mark
wann fährt der nächste Zug?	when is the next train?
um 14.20 Uhr	at 2.20 p.m.
von Gleis . . .	from platform . . .

Using public transport

1.4 WHERE DOES... LEAVE FROM?

HERR WINKLER Entschuldigung, wo fährt die Straßenbahn zur Messe ab, bitte?
PASSANT Hier geradeaus, die Haltestelle ist gegenüber dem Theater.
HERR WINKLER Ist das weit von hier?
PASSANT Nein, zwei Minuten zu Fuß.
HERR WINKLER Danke schön.

1.5 🎧 WHICH ZONE, PLEASE?

HERR WINKLER	Entschuldigen Sie bitte, ich möchte zur Messe. Welche Zone ist das?
PASSANTIN	Moment bitte, das ist nicht weit, hier, Zone 1.
HERR WINKLER	Zone 1, vielen Dank.

1.6 🎧 RETURN TICKET TO..., PLEASE

HERR WINKLER	Einmal nach Rüsselsheim bitte, hin und zurück.
BEAMTER	5,60 DM bitte.
HERR WINKLER	Entschuldigung, wieviel kostet das?
BEAMTER	Das macht 5,60 DM.
HERR WINKLER	Hier sind zehn Mark.
BEAMTER	Zehn – und 4,40 DM zurück.
HERR WINKLER	Danke. Wann fährt der nächste Zug nach Rüsselsheim, bitte?
BEAMTER	Um 14.20 Uhr von Gleis 8.
HERR WINKLER	Vielen Dank.

EXPLANATIONS AND EXERCISES

Verb forms
In this unit you have met a number of 'regular' verbs (e.g. *kosten* and *machen*) and 'irregular' verbs (e.g. *nehmen* and *fahren*). Note the endings of the regular verbs which follow the pattern below. Compare the *er, sie, es* (he, she, it) form of the irregular verbs, which must each be learnt individually.

	Regular	**Irregular**	**Irregular**
	machen to make/do	*nehmen* to take	*fahren* to go
ich er/sie/es Sie	*mache* *macht* *machen*	*nehme* **nimmt** *nehmen*	*fahre* **fährt** *fahren*

Note the important verb *sein* (to be), which is irregular throughout:

ich **bin** I am	er, sie, es **ist** he, she, it is	Sie **sind** you are

EXERCISE 1.5
Practise the verbs. Go back over dialogues 1.4 to 1.6 and highlight all of the different verb forms and the corresponding persons. Start with *fährt (die Straßenbahn)*.

Word order
Note that the verb and the person are often reversed in a question:

***Ich komme** zum Hotel.* (normal word order)
*Wie **komme ich** zum Hotel?* (question)

EXERCISE 1.6
Assume the role of Herr Winkler. Can you work out what he wants to ask? Read the responses first.

HERR WINKLER	Wie / ist / weit / zum / es /, bitte / Flughafen /?
TAXIFAHRER	Oh, das ist weit, etwa fünfundvierzig Kilometer.
HERR WINKLER	Entschuldigen / bitte / Sie /, wie / zur / ich / komme / Messe /?
PASSANT	Nehmen Sie die Linie zwölf, die fährt bis zur Messe.

'Umlaut' and 'ß'
German has four letters that do not exist in English: *ä, ö, ü* and *ß*. The two dots over the vowels, called an *Umlaut*, modify the vowel sound. The *ß* stands for *ss*:

fährt; bitte schön; fünfzig; Straßenbahn; zu Fuß.

Capital letters
In German all nouns (e.g. *die Messe*) begin with a capital letter. *Sie* also has a capital when it means 'you'.

EXERCISE 1.7
Rewrite the passage below. Capitalize where necessary. Then compare your solution with dialogue 1.4.

HERR WINKLER	entschuldigung, wo fährt die straßenbahn zur messe ab, bitte?
PASSANT	hier geradeaus, die haltestelle ist gegenüber dem theater.
HERR WINKLER	ist das weit von hier?
PASSANT	nein, zwei minuten zu fuß.
HERR WINKLER	danke schön.

EXERCISE 1.8 🎧

Listen to dialogue 1.6 again and find out the correct information.

1 What is Herr Winkler buying?

a a return ticket, 1st class **c** a return ticket, 2nd class
b a single ticket, 1st class **d** a single ticket, 2nd class

2 How much change does he get back when he buys his ticket?

a 14,20 DM **c** 5,60 DM
b 44 DM **d** 4,40 DM

3 When does the next train to Rüsselsheim leave?

a 2.20 p.m. **c** 8 p.m.
b 2.40 p.m. **d** 3.40 p.m.

EXERCISE 1.9 🎧

Listen to dialogues 1.7, 1.8 and 1.9 (tape only). Can you make sense of the directions? Try to complete the map below. You may wish to listen to each dialogue several times.

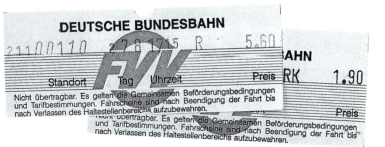

WORTH KNOWING

Travelling by public transport

In most instances German public transport is efficient and reliable. In order to find your way around you need to recognize the following signs:

- **U** (white on blue) underground *(die U-Bahn* or *Untergrundbahn)*
- **S** (white on green) fast city and suburban railway *(die S-Bahn* or *Schnellbahn)*
- **H** (green on yellow) bus or tram stop *(die Haltestelle)*
- **DB** (white on black) German railway *(die Deutsche Bundesbahn)*
- **HBF** mainline station *(der Hauptbahnhof)*

When you use the underground, city railway, bus or tram you are expected to buy your ticket in advance, usually from a ticket machine at mainline stations or from a nearby tobacconist. It is essential that you date-stamp your ticket *before* you board the underground or city railway. You usually find the machines at the top of the stairs leading down to the platforms. It is not possible to buy a ticket on an underground or city train. On some buses and trams you can buy your ticket from the driver. You then have to date-stamp it inside the bus or tram.

Railway tickets (for journeys within a range of 60 km) are also available from machines. Watch out for the sign *Fahrausweise* or *Fahrscheine* (tickets).

Travelling times are given using the 24-hour clock as, for example, in dialogue 1.6: *vierzehn Uhr zwanzig* (14.20). Colloquially you hear *zwanzig nach zwei*.

Taking a taxi
If you are not near a *Taxistand* (taxi rank), in front of a station or in the city centre it is best to call the *Taxizentrale* (taxi centre). Hailing a taxi on the move rarely works. You need to tell the controller the pick-up point, your name and your destination:

Ein Taxi zum Pichler Hof, bitte.
A taxi to the Pichler Hof, please.
Mein Name ist Landwehr, und ich möchte zum Hotel Gerau.
My name is Landwehr and I'd like to go to Hotel Gerau.

If you need a receipt for your expenses you ask for a *Quittung*: *Kann ich bitte eine Quittung haben?*
You tip the driver by adding roughly ten per cent.

Negative responses
Some inquiries will not yield a positive response simply because you have asked the wrong person. Likewise you need to be able to give a negative answer in case someone asks you for directions. Here are some examples:

Tut mir leid, ich bin auch nicht von hier.
Sorry, I'm not from here either.
Nein, keine Ahnung, tut mir leid.
No, haven't got a clue, sorry.

Help!

In order to make people slow down and repeat a sentence, you can say:

Bitte sprechen Sie langsamer!
Could you speak more slowly, please?
Bitte wiederholen Sie das!
Could you repeat that, please?

Or as a last resort:

Ich verstehe Sie nicht, ich bin Ausländer (m.)/*Ausländerin* (f.).
I don't understand, I'm a foreigner.

SELF-ASSESSMENT

You will get a rough indication of how well you're doing by filling in the guide below:

	from memory (A)	with some reference to the text (B)	with full support (C)
I can recognize a number of signs and places			
I can understand simple directions			
I can understand numbers up to 100			
I can ask the way to various destinations			
I can repeat simple directions			
I can give simple directions			

If you have ticked mostly As you are doing well. If there are quite a few Cs you'd better take your book with you.

2 INTRODUCTIONS

● ABOUT UNIT 2 ●

In this unit you'll learn how to get through to the right person on the phone, how to make and cancel an appointment, and how to introduce yourself both on the phone and in a business meeting. You'll also learn a few useful phrases for the initial contact with a new business partner, and train your ear to pick up simple messages on the answerphone.

● MAKING AN APPOINTMENT ●

KEY WORDS AND PHRASES	
guten Tag	hallo
mein Name ist . . .	my name is . . .
ich möchte Herrn/Frau . . . sprechen	I would like to talk to Mr/Mrs/Miss/Ms . . .
(es) tut mir leid	I'm sorry
im Moment	at the moment/at present
die Besprechung (-en)	meeting
er/sie ist in einer Besprechung	he/she is in a meeting
kann ich Ihnen helfen?	can I help you?
ich rufe später noch mal an	I'll call back later
auf Wiederhören	goodbye (on the phone)
die Einkaufsabteilung (-en)	purchasing department

der Einkauf (-)	purchasing department
ich verbinde	I'll put you through
ich möchte einen Termin mit Herrn Klein vereinbaren	I'd like to make an appointment with Mr Klein
wie war der Name, bitte?	what was your name again?
können Sie das bitte buchstabieren?	could you spell that, please?
paßt es Ihnen (am) Donnerstag?	would Thursday suit you?
um 10.30 Uhr	at 10.30 a.m.
das geht	that's okay

gleich (handwritten)

Telephone appointments

2.1 🎧 MY NAME IS...

SEKRETÄRIN	Hartwig & Klein, guten Tag.
HERR KRÜGER	Guten Tag, mein Name ist Krüger. Ich möchte bitte Herrn Klein sprechen.
SEKRETÄRIN	Tut mir leid, Herr Klein ist im Moment in einer Besprechung. Kann ich Ihnen helfen?
HERR KRÜGER	Nein, vielen Dank, ich rufe später noch mal an. Auf Wiederhören.
SEKRETÄRIN	Auf Wiederhören.

2.2 🎧 I'D LIKE TO MAKE AN APPOINTMENT FOR...

ZENTRALE	Hartwig & Klein, guten Tag.
FRAU SEIFERT	Guten Tag, die Einkaufsabteilung, bitte.
ZENTRALE	Moment bitte, ich verbinde.
SEKRETÄRIN	Einkauf, Neuberger.
FRAU SEIFERT	Guten Tag, VEM Dresden, mein Name ist Seifert. Ich möchte einen Termin mit Herrn Klein vereinbaren.

SEKRETÄRIN	Ja, wie war der Name, bitte?
FRAU SEIFERT	Seifert.
SEKRETÄRIN	Können Sie das bitte buchstabieren?
FRAU SEIFERT	Siegfried – Emil – Ida – Friedrich – Emil – Richard – Theodor.
SEKRETÄRIN	Frau Seifert, paßt es Ihnen Donnerstag, 10.30 Uhr?
FRAU SEIFERT	Ja, das geht. Vielen Dank.

EXPLANATIONS AND EXERCISES

The 24-hour clock

When making a business appointment, most people use the 24-hour clock in order to distinguish between morning and afternoon appointments:

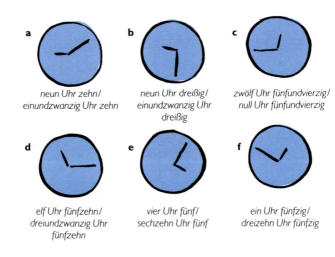

a *neun Uhr zehn/ einundzwanzig Uhr zehn*

b *neun Uhr dreißig/ einundzwanzig Uhr dreißig*

c *zwölf Uhr fünfundvierzig/ null Uhr fünfundvierzig*

d *elf Uhr fünfzehn/ dreiundzwanzig Uhr fünfzehn*

e *vier Uhr fünf/ sechzehn Uhr fünf*

f *ein Uhr fünfzig/ dreizehn Uhr fünfzig*

In everyday use you hear:

halb eins	=	half past **twelve**!
Viertel vor/nach	=	a quarter to/past
zehn vor/nach	=	ten to/past

EXERCISE 2.1
Can you match the colloquial times below with the 'official' ones above?

1 *Viertel vor eins*
2 *zehn vor zwei*
3 *zehn nach neun*
4 *Viertel nach elf*
5 *halb zehn*
6 *fünf nach vier*

The telephone alphabet 🎧
On the telephone, business people often use easy-to-understand names when spelling a name or place that may be difficult to catch otherwise. Practise the names of the telephone alphabet and try to learn as many as possible. You'll find them in your pronunciation guide at the beginning of tape 2.

A	Anton	**K**	Kaufmann	**ß**	scharfes s
Ä	Ärger	**L**	Ludwig	**Sch**	Schule
B	Berta	**M**	Martha	**T**	Theodor
C	Cäsar	**N**	Nordpol	**U**	Ulrich
D	Dora	**O**	Otto	**Ü**	Übermut
E	Emil	**Ö**	Ökonom	**V**	Viktor
F	Friedrich	**P**	Paula	**W**	Wilhelm
G	Gustav	**Q**	Quelle	**X**	Xanthippe
H	Heinrich	**R**	Richard	**Y**	Ypsilon
I	Ida	**S**	Siegfried	**Z**	Zeppelin
J	Julius				

EXERCISE 2.2 🎧
Listen to the first section of unit 2 and write down the two names spelt by Katrin using the telephone alphabet.

EXERCISE 2.3
Spell your surname using the telephone alphabet.

TELEPHONE PHRASES

ich möchte bitte Herrn/Frau . . . sprechen	I'd like to speak to Mr/Mrs/Miss/Ms . . .
ich hätte gern Herrn/Frau . . . gesprochen	
kann ich bitte Herrn/Frau . . . sprechen?	could I speak to Mr/Mrs/Miss/Ms . . .?
bleiben Sie am Apparat	please hold the line
ich verbinde/ich stelle durch	I'll put you through
wann kann ich ihn/sie erreichen?	when can I reach him/her?
wollen Sie eine Nachricht hinterlassen?	would you like to leave a message?
ich rufe später zurück/noch mal an	I'll call back later

EXERCISE 2.4
Can you reconstruct the dialogue below? Compare your solution with dialogue 2.1.

① Kann ich Ihnen helfen?

② Hartwig & Klein, guten Tag.

③ Auf Wiederhören.

④ Ich möchte bitte Herrn Klein sprechen.

⑤ Nein, vielen Dank, ich rufe später noch mal an.

⑥ Auf Wiederhören.

⑦ Tut mir leid, Herr Klein ist im Moment in einer Besprechung.

⑧ Guten Tag, mein Name ist Krüger.

EXERCISE 2.5
You are planning to go to Germany on business. Ring the company Teubert & Wiese in Cologne and make an appointment for Tuesday next week.

SEKRETÄRIN	Teubert & Wiese.
SIE	(Say hallo and introduce yourself. Say you'd like to make an appointment with Mrs Breuer.)
SEKRETÄRIN	Ja, wie war der Name, bitte?

SIE	(Repeat your name.)
SEKRETÄRIN	Können Sie das bitte buchstabieren?
SIE	(Spell your name.)
SEKRETÄRIN	Ja, einen Moment, ich schaue mal nach. Paßt es Ihnen nächsten Dienstag? Das ist der siebzehnte.
SIE	(Say that's okay, thank her and say goodbye.)

● CANCELLING AN APPOINTMENT ●

KEY WORDS AND PHRASES

ich hatte einen Termin für . . .	I had an appointment for . . .
das stimmt	that's right
leider muß ich den Termin absagen	I'm afraid I have to cancel the appointment
Donnerstag ist nicht möglich	Thursday is not possible
leider ist etwas dazwischengekommen	unfortunately something's cropped up
können wir einen neuen Termin vereinbaren?	can we arrange a new date?
ich schaue mal nach	I'll have a look

Cancelling an appointment

2.3 🎧 I HAVE TO CANCEL THE APPOINTMENT

SEKRETÄRIN	Hartwig & Klein, guten Tag.
FRAU SEIFERT	Guten Tag, Seifert, VEM Dresden. Ich hatte einen Termin mit Herrn Klein für Donnerstag um 10.30 Uhr.

SEKRETÄRIN	Ja, das stimmt.
FRAU SEIFERT	Leider muß ich den Termin absagen.
SEKRETÄRIN	Donnerstag ist nicht möglich?
FRAU SEIFERT	Nein, leider ist etwas dazwischengekommen. Können wir einen neuen Termin vereinbaren?
SEKRETÄRIN	Moment, ich schaue mal nach . . .

EXPLANATIONS AND EXERCISES

More about 'the' and 'a'
The articles 'the' and 'a' change according to gender and case.

Case	Masculine	Feminine	Neuter
Nominative (subject)	der/ein	die/eine	das/ein
Accusative (direct object)	den/einen	die/eine	das/ein
Dative (indirect object)	dem/einem	der/einer	dem/einem

*Leider muß ich **den** Termin absagen. (der Termin, m.)*
*Ich möchte **einen** Termin mit Herrn Klein vereinbaren.*
*Herr Klein ist im Moment in **einer** Besprechung. (die Besprechung, f.)*

EXERCISE 2.6

Do you remember this dialogue from unit 1? Can you fill in the appropriate form of the article 'the' or 'a'?

Entschuldigen Sie bitte, gibt es hier _____ Bank in der Nähe?
Ja, gehen Sie geradeaus, dann an _____ Restaurant links, die Bank ist neben _____ Kiosk.

COMMON EXCUSES	
er/sie ist leider im Moment außer Hause	I am sorry, he/she is not in the office at the moment
die Leitung/der Apparat ist im Moment besetzt	the line is engaged at the moment
er/sie spricht auf der anderen Leitung	he's/she's on the other line
das geht leider nicht	I'm afraid that's not possible

● FACE-TO-FACE INTRODUCTIONS (1) ●

KEY WORDS AND PHRASES	
ich habe einen Termin	I have an appointment
wenn Sie einen Moment Platz nehmen wollen	if you would like to take a seat for a moment
Herr Klein kommt Sie gleich abholen	Mr Klein will be with you shortly
wie geht es Ihnen?	how are you?
gut, danke, und Ihnen?	I'm fine, thank you, and you?
ausgezeichnet	splendid
hatten Sie eine gute Reise?	did you have a good journey?
kein Problem	no problem
gehen wir gleich in mein Büro	let's go straight to my office

Face-to-face introductions (1)

2.4 I HAVE AN APPOINTMENT WITH...

FRAU GRUBE	Guten Tag, kann ich Ihnen helfen?
FRAU SEIFERT	Ja, mein Name ist Seifert, ich habe einen Termin mit Herrn Klein um 15.00 Uhr.
FRAU GRUBE	Moment bitte. (*telephones*) Grube hier, Rezeption, ich hab' Frau Seifert hier für Herrn Klein. Ja, gut. (*hangs up*) Wenn Sie einen Moment Platz nehmen wollen, Herr Klein kommt Sie gleich abholen.
FRAU SEIFERT	Vielen Dank.

2.5 HOW ARE YOU?

HERR KLEIN	Guten Tag, Frau Seifert. Wie geht es Ihnen?
FRAU SEIFERT	Gut, danke, und Ihnen?
HERR KLEIN	Ausgezeichnet! Hatten Sie eine gute Reise?
FRAU SEIFERT	Ja danke, kein Problem.
HERR KLEIN	Gut, gehen wir gleich in mein Büro . . .

EXPLANATIONS AND EXERCISES

Days of the week

Montag	Monday
Dienstag	Tuesday
Mittwoch	Wednesday
Donnerstag	Thursday
Freitag	Friday
Samstag	Saturday
Sonntag	Sunday

Geht's bei Ihnen **am Dienstag**?	Can you make Tuesday?
Wir holen die Waren **am Mittwoch** *ab.*	We'll pick up the goods on Wednesday.
Wir brauchen den Bericht **bis Freitag**.	We need the report by Friday.
Samstags *geschlossen.*	Closed on Saturdays.

Note that all days of the week, all months and all seasons are masculine.

Times of day

gestern	yesterday	*der Vormittag*	morning
heute	today	*der Nachmittag*	afternoon
morgen	tomorrow	*der Abend*	evening
diese Woche	this week	*nächste Woche*	next week

First, second, third, etc.

Numbers between 1 and 19 mostly add ... *te* with the exception of *erste* (first) and *dritte* (third). Numbers from 20 onwards add ... *ste*.

erste	first	*einundzwanzigste*	twenty-first
zweite	second	*zweiundzwanzigste*	twenty-second
dritte	third	*dreißigste*	thirtieth
vierte	fourth	*dreiundvierzigste*	forty-third
fünfte	fifth	*neunundneunzigste*	ninety-ninth

Written as figures (for example in dates) these endings are indicated by a full stop:

13. August – der dreizehnte August
2. September – der zweite September

The verb *haben*

Learn these different forms of the verb *haben* (to have):

ich **habe**	er, sie, es **hat**	Sie **haben**
I have	he, she, it has	you have

Learn how to ask questions with *haben*.

Haben Sie einen Prospekt? — Have you got a brochure?
Haben Sie eine Preisliste? — Have you got a price list?
Haben Sie ein Büro in London? — Have you got an office in London?

EXERCISE 2.7

You've just arrived at the Weidenbach company for a meeting with Mr Schnorr. Can you find appropriate responses?

HERR SCHNORR	Guten Tag, Herr/Frau . . ., wie geht es Ihnen?
SIE	_____
HERR SCHNORR	Sehr gut, danke. Hatten Sie eine gute Reise?
SIE	_____
HERR SCHNORR	Möchten Sie einen Kaffee?
SIE	_____

● FACE-TO-FACE INTRODUCTIONS (2) ●

KEY WORDS AND PHRASES

darf ich vorstellen	may I introduce . . .
mein Geschäftspartner (-)	my business partner (m.)
meine Geschäftspartnerin (-nen)	my business partner (f.)
(es) freut mich, Sie kennenzulernen	(I'm) pleased to meet you
sehr angenehm	pleased to meet you, too
der Verkaufsleiter (-)	sales manager (m.)
die Verkaufsleiterin (-nen)	sales manager (f.)
bei der Firma Ebenhaus	at Ebenhaus (company)

der Einkaufsleiter (-)	senior buyer (m.)
die Einkaufsleiterin (-nen)	senior buyer (f.)
der Geschäftsführer (-)	director (m.)
die Geschäftsführerin (-nen)	director (f.)
der Produktionsleiter (-)	production manager (m.)
die Produktionsleiterin (-nen)	production manager (f.)
bitte nehmen sie doch Platz	please take a seat
was kann ich für Sie tun?	what can I do for you?

Face-to-face introductions (2)

2.6 MAY I INTRODUCE...

HERR KLEIN Frau Seifert, darf ich vorstellen, das ist Frau Hartwig, meine Geschäftspartnerin.
FRAU SEIFERT Es freut mich, Sie kennenzulernen.
FRAU HARTWIG Angenehm.

2.7 PLEASED TO MEET YOU

HERR KRÜGER Guten Tag, mein Name ist Krüger. Ich bin Verkaufsleiter bei der Firma Ebenhaus in Jena.
FRAU UNRUH Es freut mich, Sie kennenzulernen, mein Name ist Unruh. Ich bin Einkaufsleiterin bei Sassen & Co. in Stuttgart.

2.8 DO TAKE A SEAT

DR. SCHREIBER Guten Tag, mein Name ist Dr. Wilhelm Schreiber. Ich bin Geschäftsführer der Firma Sietz in Köln.
HERR HUBER Freut mich, Herr Dr. Schreiber. Frank Huber, Produktionsleiter bei NAM in Frankfurt.
DR. SCHREIBER Bitte nehmen Sie doch Platz, Herr Huber. Was kann ich für Sie tun?

EXPLANATIONS AND EXERCISES

Describing your job

When someone asks you what your job is (*Was sind Sie von Beruf?*) you simply say *Ich bin* . . . followed by the name of your job, for example:

Ich bin Verkaufsleiter(in) or *Ich bin Einkaufsleiter(in)*.

To say where you work, use *bei*; to say from which company you are, use *von*:

*Ich arbeite **bei** (der Firma) Ebenhaus.*
*Ich komme **von** der Firma Meier.*

If you are the boss you say:

Ich bin Geschäftsführer(in) der Firma . . .

Talking about your company and products

Unsere Hauptgeschäftsstelle ist in . . .
Our head office is in . . .

Unsere Produkte sind von ausgezeichneter Qualität.
Our products are of outstanding quality.

Wir stellen . . . her/Wir produzieren . . . We produce . . .
Wir verkaufen . . . We sell . . .

Wir sind Marktführer auf diesem Gebiet.
We are market leaders in this area.

Wir haben einen Marktanteil von . . . Prozent.
We have a market share of . . . per cent.

EXERCISE 2.8 🎧

Listen to the two messages on the answerphone in dialogue 2.9 (tape only) and note down the names of the callers, their companies, their positions in the company, the time of the desired appointments and their phone numbers. Write your notes in English on the chart overleaf. Which caller doesn't state their position?

Name	Company	Position	Appointment	Telephone No.

WORTH KNOWING

Making an appointment
The initial contact is best made in an introductory letter written in good business German. After about a fortnight you should follow up your letter with a phone call and try to arrange a meeting. You normally fix a date for the meeting with the secretary. Formality is the key to a successful business relationship, and it is very important that you are punctual, which means on the dot. Expect the meeting to be formal and matter-of-fact.

Greetings and forms of address
Handshaking occurs on every possible occasion, at the beginning and end of a meeting or each time a newcomer is introduced. When shaking hands you can say *guten Tag* at any time of day or *angenehm* as a reply, which is short for 'pleased to meet you'. The general rule for business people is to address each other by *Herr* or *Frau* followed by their surname or, if they have one, by their title (e.g. *Dr.*) and surname. Address all women over the age of 18 as *Frau*.

The formal and informal 'you'
There are two 'you' forms in German. It is important that you select the correct one. The formal or polite form for 'you', which is always used in business, is *Sie*. The informal *du* is used between adults who know each other well, between students and children and by an adult speaking to a child. Check the above dialogues for the use of *Sie*.

Ihnen (to you) is used in connection with certain verbs and prepositions:

*Wir schicken **Ihnen** die Waren per Express.*
We'll send the goods to you by express.

*Paßt es **Ihnen** nächsten Dienstag?*
Does next Tuesday suit you?

*Wir besprechen das mit **Ihnen** in London.*
We'll discuss that with you in London.

SELF-ASSESSMENT

Tick the following categories for your self-assessment guide:

	from memory (A)	with some reference to the text (B)	with full support (C)
I can make and cancel an appointment by telephone			
I can greet people and introduce myself and others			
I can state my position in my company			
I can understand the 24-hour clock and the days of the week			
I can understand the telephone alphabet and spell my name			
I can understand simple telephone messages			

If you have ticked mostly As you are doing very well. If there are quite a few Cs, try playing your tape when stuck in that traffic jam!

3 ENQUIRIES

● ABOUT UNIT 3 ●

In unit 3 you are getting down to business. You'll learn how to make contact with a prospective customer, how to respond to an enquiry about the stock situation and how to discuss delivery times and discount terms. Finally you'll learn how to give and take down an order and ask for written confirmation of the order. And you'll manage all this on the telephone.

● MAKING CONTACT ●

KEY WORDS AND PHRASES	
wir produzieren	we produce
die Haushaltswaren (pl.)	household goods
der Geschenkartikel (-)	giftware
ich möchte Ihnen gerne unsere Produktpalette vorstellen	I'd like to present our product range to you
vielleicht	perhaps
senden/schicken Sie uns doch . . .	why don't you send us . . .
zunächst einmal	first of all
der Katalog (-e)	catalogue
die Preisliste (-n)	price list

das mache ich gerne	I'll certainly do that
darf ich Ihnen noch meine Durchwahl geben	could I just give you my number (direct line)
falls Sie irgendwelche Fragen haben	in case you have any queries
die Nummer (-n)	number

Making contact

3.1 🎧 I'D LIKE TO PRESENT OUR PRODUCT RANGE

ZENTRALE	Sassen & Co., guten Tag.
HERR KRÜGER	Guten Tag, die Einkaufsabteilung, Frau Unruh, bitte.
ZENTRALE	Einen Moment bitte, ich verbinde.
FRAU UNRUH	Unruh.
HERR KRÜGER	Guten Tag, Frau Unruh, mein Name ist Krüger von der Firma Ebenhaus in Jena. Wir produzieren Haushaltswaren und Geschenkartikel, und ich möchte Ihnen gerne einmal unsere Produktpalette vorstellen. Vielleicht könnten wir einen Termin vereinbaren . . .
FRAU UNRUH	Ja – Herr Krüger, dann schicken Sie uns doch zunächst einmal Ihren Katalog und Ihre Preisliste.
HERR KRÜGER	Das mache ich gerne. Darf ich Ihnen noch meine Durchwahl geben, falls Sie irgendwelche Fragen haben?
FRAU UNRUH	Ja, bitte.
HERR KRÜGER	Die Nummer ist (0342) 78 23 66.

EXPLANATIONS AND EXERCISES

Regular verbs
When you look up a verb in a dictionary, you'll find the 'infinitive', e.g. *produzieren* – to produce, or *machen* – to make/do. From this you can work out the different endings for the present tense: remove the verb ending (*-en*) and add the following endings to the verb stem:

produzier + *-e*   *-st*   *-t*   *-en*   *-t*   *-en*   *-en*

For example:

		produzieren	machen	senden
I	ich	produzier**e**	mach**e**	send**e**
you (informal)	du	produzier**st**	_____	send**est**
he, she, it	er, sie, es	produzier**t**	_____	send**et**
we	wir	produzier**en**	_____	send**en**
you (informal)	ihr	produzier**t**	_____	send**et**
they	sie	produzier**en**	_____	send**en**
you (formal)	Sie	produzier**en**	_____	send**en**

Note that if the stem ends in *t* or *d* (e.g. *senden* – to send, or *kosten* – to cost) the endings are:

send + *-e*   *-est*   *-et*   *-en*   *-et*   *-en*   *-en*

EXERCISE 3.1
Complete the table above with *machen*.

You may find it helpful to revise your verb table in unit 1.

The verbs *sein* and *haben*
You have already met some of the forms of *sein* (to be) and *haben* (to have) in units 1 and 2. These verbs are irregular throughout and you need to learn them carefully.

		sein	haben
I	ich	bin	habe
you (informal)	du	bist	hast
he, she, it	er, sie, es	ist	hat
we	wir	sind	haben
you (informal)	ihr	seid	habt
they	sie	sind	haben
you (formal)	Sie	sind	haben

EXERCISE 3.2
Complete the dialogue below using the correct forms of *sein* and *haben*.

HERR KRÜGER	Mein Name _____ Krüger, ich _____ Produktionsleiter bei NAM in Frankfurt. Ich _____ einen Termin mit Frau Unruh um 10.30 Uhr.
SEKRETÄRIN	Es tut mir leid, sie _____ noch in einer Besprechung. Sie _____ ein wenig zu früh (*a little too early*). Bitte nehmen Sie einen Moment Platz.

EXERCISE 3.3
Listen to dialogue 3.1 again, assume the role of Herr Krüger, and make a note of the following information in English:

Notes
Company:
Contact name:
Department:
Action:

SEEKING BUSINESS CONTACTS

Wir suchen einen Partner für den Vertrieb von . . .
We are seeking a partner for the sale and distribution of . . .

Wir suchen einen Handelsvertreter.
We are looking for an agent.

Wir bieten die folgenden Dienstleistungen an: . . .
We offer the following services: . . .

Wir haben ausgezeichnete Kontakte zu allen größeren Verkaufsstellen.
We have excellent contacts with all major outlets.

Asking for a catalogue

3.2   COULD YOU PLEASE SEND US . . .

This dialogue is on tape only. Read the task below and then listen to dialogue 3.2.

EXERCISE 3.4
You're working for Mills Pharmaceuticals in London and have seen the advertisement below in *British–German Trade*. Ring the company and ask them to send you a catalogue and a price list.

TRADE ENQUIRIES FROM GERMANY

. . . a wide range of quality packagings of excellent design and finish for the pharmaceutical industry . . . contact Frau Heike Bruck, Sales, Kalden GmbH, Tel. (010 49) 5655-87 12 22.

ENQUIRING ABOUT THE STOCK SITUATION

KEY WORDS AND PHRASES	
Sie erinnern sich?	do you recall?
natürlich	of course
schön, daß Sie anrufen	good of you to call
wir interessieren uns für . . .	we are interested in . . .
der Artikel (-)	item
aus Ihrem Katalog	from your catalogue
der Espresso-Automat (-en)/ die Espresso-Maschine (-n)	espresso machine
der Entsafter (-)	juice extractor
haben Sie diese Produkte vorrätig?	do you have these products in stock?
da muß ich mit unserem Lager sprechen	well, I'll have to talk to our warehouse
an welche Größenordnung hatten Sie gedacht?	what amount were you thinking of?
etwa	about, approximately
das ist in Ordnung	that's okay

Enquiring about the stock situation

3.3 🎧 HAVE YOU GOT THESE PRODUCTS IN STOCK?

HERR KRÜGER	Krüger.
FRAU UNRUH	Guten Tag, Herr Krüger. Mein Name ist Unruh von der Firma Sassen & Co. Sie erinnern sich?
HERR KRÜGER	Ja, natürlich, Frau Unruh; schön, daß Sie anrufen. Wie kann ich Ihnen helfen?
FRAU UNRUH	Wir interessieren uns für zwei Artikel aus

	Ihrem Katalog, die Espresso-Automaten und die Entsafter. Haben Sie diese Produkte vorrätig?
HERR KRÜGER	Da muß ich mit unserem Lager sprechen. An welche Größenordnung hatten Sie gedacht?
FRAU UNRUH	Etwa 150 Espresso-Automaten und 80 Entsafter.
HERR KRÜGER	Darf ich Sie gleich zurückrufen?
FRAU UNRUH	Ja, das ist in Ordnung. Wiederhören.
HERR KRÜGER	Wiederhören.

EXPLANATIONS AND EXERCISES

More about verbs

A small group of verbs (modal verbs) are not complete on their own. They almost always need to be completed by an infinitive at the end of the sentence. Here are some examples from the dialogues:

*Ich **möchte** Ihnen unsere Produktpalette **vorstellen**.*
*Ich **muß** mit unserem Lager **sprechen**.*
***Darf** ich Sie gleich **zurückrufen**?*
***Kann** ich Ihnen **helfen**?*

EXERCISE 3.5

How would you translate the following phrases?

a I'd like to speak to Mr Kaufmann, please.

b I'm afraid I have to cancel the appointment.

c May I call you back tomorrow?

d When can I reach him?

'My' and 'your'

You've already used the possessive *mein/meine* (my) and *Ihr/Ihre* (formal: your) in a number of different situations:

*Wie ist **Ihr** Name?* (m.)
What's your name?

***Mein** Name ist* . . . (m.)
My name is . . .

*Wie ist **Ihre** Telefonnummer?* (f.)
What's your phone number?

***Meine** Telefonnummer* . . . (f.)
My phone number is . . .

*Wo ist **Ihr** Hotel?* (n.)
Where is your hotel?

***Mein** Hotel ist* . . . (n.)
My hotel is . . .

You may have noticed other endings on *mein* and *Ihr*. After most verbs you use *Ihren* with masculine nouns, *Ihre* with feminine and *Ihr* with neuter nouns (e.g. when they're the direct object).

*Schicken Sie uns doch **Ihren** Katalog und **Ihre** Preisliste.*

After some words such as *mit* and *aus* (prepositions), you use *Ihrem* with masculine and neuter nouns and *Ihrer* with feminine nouns:

*Wir interessieren uns für zwei Artikel aus **Ihrem** Katalog.*
*Bitte verbinden Sie mich mit **Ihrer** Einkaufsabteilung.*

But don't worry if you get the endings wrong. You'll still be understood.

EXERCISE 3.6
'My' or 'your'? Fill in the correct forms with the appropriate endings:

_____ Name ist Unruh von der Firma Sassen & Co. Wir interessieren uns für zwei Artikel aus _____ Katalog, die Espresso-Automaten und die Entsafter. Schicken Sie uns doch _____ Katalog und _____ Preisliste.

Ja gerne, wie ist _____ Name, _____ Adresse und _____ Telefonnummer, bitte?

EXPLANATIONS AND EXERCISES

Dates

Das ist die | Lieferung / Bestellung / Rechnung | vom | zehnten März. / vierten Oktober. / dritten Juni.

EXERCISE 4.7
You are ringing a supplier about an order. Give the dispatch department the requested information.

a *Ja, haben Sie das Bestelldatum, bitte?*
   (Say it's the order of 10 June.)
b *Ja, haben Sie das Rechnungsdatum, bitte?*
   (Say it's the invoice of 7 May.)
c *Ja, haben Sie das Lieferdatum?*
   (Say it's the delivery of 13 December.)

Deadlines

Wir brauchen | die Lieferung / den Bericht / das Modell | (spätestens) bis / (spätestens) am | Freitag. / 19. August. / Montag, den 1. Juni.

EXERCISE 4.8
Impress upon your supplier that you need certain goods or documents on the stipulated date.

a We need the delivery on Tuesday, 28 March at the latest.
b We need the report on Wednesday.
c We need the machines by 21 April.

EXERCISE 4.9 🎧
Can you spot the mistakes on Frau Krause's memo to Herr Kluge overleaf? First listen again to dialogue 4.3.

Frau Krause cannot send out the urgent delivery as she is

about to leave for a training seminar. She leaves her colleague some notes to act upon. Because she is in a hurry, she makes a few mistakes.

> ### *Herr Kluge*
>
> - *Computech in Bonn – Lieferung noch nicht erhalten*
> - *Bestellung vom 4.1. – Modem V22*
> - *Bestellnummer: F–905367–ER*
> - *Lieferung bitte ersetzen – Modems vorrätig*
> - *Lieferung spätestens in 14 Tagen*
>
> *Bitte veranlassen*

● DELIVERY PROBLEMS (2) ●

KEY WORDS AND PHRASES

die Lieferung ist gerade angekommen	the delivery has just arrived
Sie haben uns die falsche Menge geschickt	you've sent us the incorrect quantity
anstatt	instead of
die Lieferscheine fehlen	the delivery papers are missing
das ist wirklich sehr ärgerlich	that's a real nuisance
der Fehler (-)	mistake
der Rest (-e)	rest
per Express	express delivery
äußerst dringend	extremely urgent
durchfaxen	to fax through

Delivery problems (2)

4.4 🎧 YOU'VE SENT US THE INCORRECT QUANTITY

FRAU FINK	Frau Krause, Ihre Lieferung ist gerade angekommen, aber Sie haben uns die falsche Menge geschickt, nur 30 anstatt 50 Stück! Und die Lieferscheine fehlen! Das ist wirklich sehr ärgerlich.
FRAU KRAUSE	Einen Moment, bitte, ich schaue mal nach. – Oh, das tut mir sehr leid. Das ist mein Fehler. Wir können Ihnen den Rest per Express schicken.
FRAU FINK	Ja, es ist wirklich äußerst dringend, und faxen Sie bitte die Lieferscheine sofort durch.

EXPLANATIONS AND EXERCISES

Apologies when things go wrong

Die Maschinen funktionieren nicht.	The machines don't work.
Das tut mir leid, wir schicken Ihnen unseren Ingenieur.	I'm sorry, we'll send our engineer out to you.
Die Waren sind beschädigt.	The goods are damaged.
Das tut mir leid, wir ersetzen Ihnen die beschädigten Waren.	I'm sorry, we'll replace the damaged goods.
Die Lieferscheine fehlen.	The delivery papers are missing.
Oh, entschuldigen Sie bitte, wir faxen sie Ihnen gleich durch.	Ah, I'm sorry. We'll fax them straight through to you.

EXERCISE 4.10 🎧

What went wrong? Listen again to dialogue 4.4 and tick the right answers.

a The delivery hasn't arrived.
b The quantity is incorrect.
c The invoices are missing.
d The supplier has sent the order by express delivery.
e The delivery papers are missing.
f 30 items are damaged.

● AN OVERDUE PAYMENT ●

KEY WORDS AND PHRASES	
die Buchhaltung (-en)	accounts department
ein paar überfällige Zahlungen	a few overdue payments
können wir das kurz besprechen?	can we briefly discuss these?
erstens	first of all
zweitens	secondly
die Rechnungsnummer (-n)	invoice number
bleiben Sie bitte am Apparat	please hold the line
. . . hören Sie bitte?	. . . hallo? (re-establishing contact on the phone)
überweisen	to transfer (money)
wir haben den Betrag auf Ihr Konto überwiesen	we have transferred the amount into your account
die Zahlung ist aber bei uns noch nicht eingegangen	but we haven't received the payment yet

sie kommt bestimmt in den nächsten Tagen	I'm sure you'll receive it within the next few days
eine Rechnung begleichen	to settle an invoice
wir haben die Rechnung beglichen	we've settled the invoice
dann haben wir alles geklärt	that's everything settled, then

An overdue payment

4.5 🎧 THERE ARE A FEW OVERDUE PAYMENTS

FRAU ARNDT Buchhaltung, Arndt.
FRAU FINK Guten Morgen, Frau Arndt. Ich hab' hier ein paar überfällige Zahlungen, können wir das kurz besprechen?
FRAU ARNDT Ja, natürlich – da brauche ich von Ihnen Rechnungsnummer und Datum.
FRAU FINK Also, da ist erstens die Rechnungsnummer KA–734569 vom 9.12.
FRAU ARNDT Ja.
FRAU FINK . . . und zweitens die Rechnungsnummern VB–90367 und VB–90368, beide vom 17.12.
FRAU ARNDT Moment, ich hole mir die Akte, bleiben Sie bitte am Apparat.
FRAU FINK Ja, danke, ich warte . . .
FRAU ARNDT . . . Frau Fink, hören Sie bitte? Den Betrag für die Rechnung vom 9.12. haben wir am 12.1. auf Ihr Konto überwiesen.
FRAU FINK Die Zahlung ist aber bei uns noch nicht eingegangen.
FRAU ARNDT Sie kommt bestimmt in den nächsten Tagen. Die Rechnungen vom 17. Dezember haben wir gestern beglichen.
FRAU FINK Gut, dann haben wir alles geklärt. Ich danke Ihnen.
FRAU ARNDT Bitte schön. Wiederhören.

EXPLANATIONS AND EXERCISES

EXERCISE 4.11 🎧
Listen to dialogue 4.5 and tick the main reason for Frau Fink's call.

a She wants to check two invoice numbers.
b She wants to pay two overdue payments.
c She wants to chase up a few overdue payments.

Make a note of the three invoice numbers and dates.

Verbs with *haben* and *sein*
To talk about the past, the verbs *haben* or *sein* (auxiliaries) are used with a form of the main verb (past participle) in spoken German. Compare the following sentences:

I **have spoken** to the boss.
*Ich **habe** mit dem Chef **gesprochen**.*

The delivery **has arrived**.
*Die Lieferung **ist angekommen**.*

Here are some more examples from the dialogues:

*Wir **haben** den Betrag **überwiesen**.*
*Er **hat** die Zahlung **beglichen**.*
*Sie **haben** alles **geklärt**.*

Verbs that imply a change of place or state normally form the perfect tense with *sein*:

*Die Lieferung **ist** noch nicht **angekommen**.*
*Die Zahlungen **sind** bei uns nicht **eingegangen**.*

EXERCISE 4.12

You've had a number of problems at the office. Tell your colleague what went wrong and how you solved the problems.

SIE	(The delivery arrived too late *(zu spät)*. They've sent us the wrong amount. We haven't received the payments yet.)
KOLLEGE	*Und was haben Sie gemacht?*
SIE	(I've talked to the boss. They've sent us a replacement delivery. They've settled the invoice. We've solved the problems.)

EXERCISE 4.13

Ring back Frau Fink and tell her:

a you've got good news for her
b you transferred the overdue payments into her firm's account on 12 January.

EXERCISE 4.14

Do you remember how to stall someone when you can't or don't wish to give an immediate reply?

Frau Arndt says: *Ich hole mir die Akte und rufe Sie dann zurück.*

What else could you say in her situation? You'll find some answers in unit 3.

WORTH KNOWING

Complaints

If goods are damaged or defective in any way, the purchaser has three options under German law: to withdraw from the contract (*Rückgängigmachung des Kaufvertrags*); to ask for a reduction of the purchasing price (*Minderung des Kaufpreises*); or to insist on a delivery of perfect goods (*auf mangelfreier Lieferung bestehen*). In order to make absolutely sure what your rights are, ask a lawyer to check the small print of the terms of trade (*die allgemeinen Geschäftsbedingungen*) before you enter into a contract.

If there is a problem or a dispute, have a word with the manager. You can say: *Ich möchte den Geschäftsführer sprechen.* This usually has the desired effect of sending shivers down the *Sachbearbeiter's* spine, and things normally run smoothly from then onwards.

TERMS OF PAYMENT

die Zahlungsbedingungen (pl.)	payment terms
die Zahlungsaufforderung (-en)	request for payment
Zahlung innerhalb (von) 30 Tagen	payment within 30 days
Zahlung gegen Rechnung	payment against invoice
Zahlung 15 Tage ab Rechnungsdatum: drei Prozent Skonto	for payment made within 15 days from date of invoice: three per cent discount

Invoices

Germans become irritated when invoices are not paid on time, and you can expect to pay both a fee for reminders (*Mahngebühr*) and, once a deadline has been set for an overdue payment, interest (*Verzugszinsen*) on the overdue amount. For more details on reminders, see unit 5.

SELF-ASSESSMENT

Tick the following categories for your self-assessment guide:

	from memory (A)	with some reference to the text (B)	with full support (C)
I can make a simple complaint and ask to get something checked			
I can understand a complaint and respond to it, ask for more details or stall if necessary			
I can apologize when things have gone wrong and tell the customer that appropriate action will be taken			
I can understand dates and invoice numbers on the telephone and make a note of them			
I can report back on delivery and payment problems			
I can urge someone to deliver goods or documents by a specified date			

Are you still awarding yourself mostly As, or have you recently moved up into that category? Carry on, you're doing fine. If not, spend some time on revision before carrying on.

5 COPING WITH CORRESPONDENCE

● ABOUT UNIT 5 ●

In this unit you'll look at a number of simple written documents. You'll learn to understand and check a confirmation of an order sent by fax, and what to say if any of the details are incorrect. You'll be able to read and write a straightforward hotel reservation, study an invoice and get to grips with special terminology and abbreviations. Furthermore, you'll gain practice in extracting the main points of a business letter about production problems.

● ACKNOWLEDGEMENT OF ORDER (1) ●

KEY WORDS AND PHRASES

die Auftragsbestätigung (-en)	acknowledgement of order
Sie haben gerade . . . durchgefaxt	you have just faxed through . . .
die Kopie (-n)	copy
schlecht	bad
die Stückzahl (-en)	number of items
der Liefertermin (-e)	delivery date
die Zahlungsbedingungen (pl.)	payment terms

Acknowledgement of order

5.1 COULD YOU CONFIRM...

HERR KRÜGER	Krüger.
FRAU UNRUH	Guten Tag, Herr Krüger, Unruh von der Firma Sassen & Co.
HERR KRÜGER	Tag, Frau Unruh, was kann ich für Sie tun?
FRAU UNRUH	Sie haben gerade eine Auftragsbestätigung durchgefaxt. Leider ist die Kopie sehr schlecht. Könnten Sie noch einmal die genauen Stückzahlen, Liefertermine und Zahlungsbedingungen bestätigen?
HERR KRÜGER	Ja sicher, einen Moment – das sind die 150 Espresso-Automaten für Woche 23 und 100 Entsafter zum 1. Dezember. Alles frei Haus mit drei Prozent Mengenrabatt.
FRAU UNRUH	Ja, richtig.
HERR KRÜGER	Das geht in Ordnung, Frau Unruh, ich faxe die Auftragsbestätigung gleich noch mal durch.

ACKNOWLEDGEMENT OF ORDER (2)

KEY WORDS AND PHRASES

die (Tele-)Faxnachricht (-en)	fax message
unser/Ihr Zeichen	our/your reference
Ihre Nachricht vom . . .	your letter of . . .
Anzahl der zu übermittelnden Seiten	number of (transmitted) pages
die Bestellmenge (-n)	quantity ordered
die Liefermenge (-n)	quantity delivered
die Artikel-Nummer (-n)	product code
die Artikel-Bezeichnung (-en)	product description
der Einzelpreis (-e)	unit price
gesamt	total
MwSt Schl. = Mehrwertsteuer Schlüssel	VAT code
einschließlich	including
ausschließlich	excluding
die Verpackung (-en)	packaging
die Versicherung (-en)	insurance
mit freundlichen Grüßen	yours sincerely

5.1a FAX MESSAGE

FAX-NACHRICHT

Von: Firma Ebenhaus
Auerbachstraße 312
O-6900 Jena

An: Firma Sassen & Co. **Datum:** 30.9.19 ...
Frau E. Unruh
Am Bahnhof 3
W-7000 Stuttgart 1

Unser Zeichen: HK/AL **Ihre Nachricht vom:**
Anzahl der zu übermittelnden Seiten: 1 28. September 19 ...

Sehr geehrte Frau Unruh,

Auftragsbestätigung

wir danken Ihnen für den Auftrag vom 28.9. und liefern wie vereinbart:

Bestell-menge	Liefer-menge	Artikel-Nr	Artikel-Bezeichnung	Einzelpreis DM	gesamt DM	MwSt Schl.
150	150	2-298-334	Espresso-Automaten	74,00	11 100	1
100	100	5-198-223	Entsafter	82,60	8 260	1

Zahlung:
-/. 3% Skonto bei Zahlung innerhalb von 10 Tagen nach Rechnungsdatum.

Versand:
Der Versand erfolgt frei Haus, einschließlich Verpackung, ausschließlich Versicherung.

Mit freundlichen Grüßen,

H. Krüger

EXPLANATIONS AND EXERCISES

Separable verbs

Many verbs in German have prefixes such as *ab-*, *an-*, *vor-*, which separate from the main verb in main clauses:

*Wo **fährt** die Straßenbahn **ab**?*	Where does the tram leave from?
*Ich **rufe** gleich **zurück**.*	I'll call back shortly.

You've already used the following separable verbs in units 1–5:

ab/fahren	leave (from)	*durch/faxen*	fax through
ab/holen	pick up	*durch/geben*	phone through
ab/sagen	cancel	*durch/stellen*	put through
an/bieten	offer	*ein/gehen*	receive (payment)
an/kommen	arrive	*vor/stellen*	introduce
an/rufen	call	*zurück/rufen*	call back

EXERCISE 5.1
The managing director of your German subsidiary is ringing your office and wishes to participate in an important meeting.

a Ask the secretary to put the call (*das Gespräch*) through.
b Tell him you are picking him up from the airport.
c Tell him you are faxing the agenda (*die Tagesordnung*) through to him.
d There is an urgent call on the other line. Tell him you'll ring back later.

EXERCISE 5.2
Can you make sense of the following dialogue? Fill the gaps with the appropriate preposition *für, von, in, nach, bei*.

HERR HUBER	Ich bin Produktionsleiter der Firma NAM ____ Frankfurt.
DR. SCHREIBER	Guten Tag, was kann ich ____ Sie tun?
HERR HUBER	Ich möchte gern Ihre Zahlungsbedingungen wissen.
DR. SCHREIBER	Wir bieten Ihnen drei Prozent Skonto ____ Zahlung innerhalb ____ 30 Tagen ____ Rechnungsdatum.

EXERCISE 5.3 🎧
Listen to dialogue 5.1 again and compare the information requested with the acknowledgement of order sent by fax.

a Does the fax confirm: the quantity ordered? | Yes/No
the delivery dates? | Yes/No

b Compare the payment terms stated by Herr Krüger in the dialogue with the ones given on the fax. Make a note of both terms in German.
Agreed terms: _____
Stated on fax: _____

c Check the delivery terms on the fax.
The delivery: is carriage-free | Yes/No
includes insurance | Yes/No
includes packaging | Yes/No

Complaining about mistakes
When you ring back to complain about mistakes, you can state what's wrong or missing, for example:

Die Lieferbedingungen stimmen nicht.	The delivery terms are incorrect.
Der Rechnungsbetrag stimmt nicht.	The amount on the invoice is incorrect.
Die Lieferscheine fehlen.	The delivery papers are missing.
Das Rechnungsdatum fehlt.	The date on the invoice is missing.

Or you could simply say 'we had agreed . . . and not . . .':

Wir hatten drei Prozent Mengenrabatt vereinbart und nicht 2,5%.

• AN UNSUCCESSFUL BOOKING •

KEY WORDS AND PHRASES	
wir haben gerade Ihren Brief erhalten	we have just received your letter
die Zimmerreservierung	room reservation
wir sind für diese Zeit schon voll belegt	we are already fully booked on these dates
was machen wir denn da?	what do you suggest we do?
können Sie . . . empfehlen?	can you recommend . . . ?
versuchen Sie es mal . . .	you could try . . .
das ist sehr freundlich	that's very kind

An unsuccessful booking

5.2　WE ARE ALREADY FULLY BOOKED

SEKRETÄRIN	Hartwig & Klein, guten Tag.
ANGESTELLTER	Hotel Balle in Stuttgart, guten Tag. Wir haben gerade Ihren Brief erhalten. Leider können wir die Zimmerreservierung nicht bestätigen. Wir sind für diese Zeit schon voll belegt.
SEKRETÄRIN	Hm, was machen wir denn da? Können Sie uns ein Hotel in der Nähe empfehlen?
ANGESTELLTER	Ja, versuchen Sie es mal im Hotel Hofgarten, die Nummer ist (0711) 33 09 82.
SEKRETÄRIN	Vielen Dank, das ist sehr freundlich.

● HOTEL RESERVATION ●

KEY WORDS AND PHRASES

reservieren	to reserve
ein Einzelzimmer mit Dusche	a single room with shower
zum Preis von	at (a price of)
pro Übernachtung	per night
Adresse obenstehend	at the above address
die Buchung (-en)	booking
i.A. = im Auftrag	p.p. (on behalf of)

5.2a BOOKING A SINGLE ROOM

Hartwig & Klein
seit 1925

Bundesallee 88 D-1000 Berlin 15 Tel. (030) 29 28 55 Fax (030) 29 28 56

Hotel Balle
Botenstraße 108-110
7000 Stuttgart 1

Ihr Zeichen	Ihre Nachricht vom	Unser Zeichen	Datum
		HK/KL	12.09. ...

Sehr geehrte Damen und Herren,

Zimmerreservierung

bitte reservieren Sie für Montag und Dienstag, den 25. und 26. September 19... ein Einzelzimmer mit Dusche/WC zum Preis von 129.-DM pro Übernachtung für Herrn Klein, Adresse obenstehend.

Bitte bestätigen Sie die Buchung so bald wie möglich.

Mit freundlichen Grüßen,

i. A. Karen Landwehr

EXPLANATIONS AND EXERCISES

EXERCISE 5.4 🎧

Listen to dialogue 5.2 and decide on the main reason for the call from Hotel Balle in Stuttgart.

a to confirm the booking
b to query the details of the booking
c to inform the secretary that they are fully booked

EXERCISE 5.5 🎧

Read Frau Landwehr's letter to Hotel Balle. When she books a room in a different hotel, she has to agree to some changes in the booking. Listen to the dialogue (tape only), find out what they are, and inform Herr Klein of the changes.

a room: **b** price:

BOOKING A HOTEL ROOM	
ich hätte gern ein Zimmer reserviert	I'd like to book a room
auf welchen Namen?	in what name?
das Doppelzimmer (-)	double room
vom 7. bis 10. . . .	from the 7th to the 10th . . .
für zwei Nächte	for two nights
würden Sie sich bitte hier eintragen	would you please sign the register here

EXERCISE 5.6

You've just seen an advertisement for Hotel Wiese in a travel brochure (opposite above). Write a short letter booking a single room with bath and WC for two nights from 12–14 February. Ask them to confirm the booking as soon as possible.

WIESE

IHR HOTEL IM STADTZENTRUM
Bahnhofstraße 3, 7000 Stuttgart 1

● QUERYING AN INVOICE (1) ●

KEY WORDS AND PHRASES

glauben	to think/believe
Sie haben unseren Kundenrabatt nicht von der Rechnung abgezogen	you haven't deducted our customer discount from the invoice
Sie haben recht	you are right
das haben wir leider übersehen	I'm sorry, it's an oversight on our part
eine berichtigte Kopie	an amended copy
ich bitte um Entschuldigung	I beg your pardon

Querying an invoice (1)

5.3 I THINK THE AMOUNT IS INCORRECT

FRAU ARNDT Buchhaltung, Arndt.
FRAU FINK Guten Morgen, Frau Arndt. Ich habe gerade Ihre Rechnung vom 2.7. erhalten. Ich glaube, der Rechnungsbetrag stimmt nicht. Sie haben unseren Kundenrabatt von fünf Prozent nicht von der Rechnung abgezogen.
FRAU ARNDT Oh. Ich überprüfe das gleich, Frau Fink, bleiben Sie einen Moment am Apparat . . . Mm. Frau Fink.
. . . hören Sie bitte? Sie haben recht, das haben wir leider übersehen. Wir schicken

	Ihnen eine berichtigte Kopie der Rechnung zu. Ich bitte um Entschuldigung.
FRAU FINK	Das ist in Ordnung, Frau Arndt. Wiederhören.
FRAU ARNDT	Auf Wiederhören.

● QUERYING AN INVOICE (2) ●

KEY WORDS AND PHRASES

die Anzahl (-)	number
die Kundennummer (-n)	customer number
die Versandart (-en)	method of dispatch

5.3a YOUR ORDER OF...

NAM PARTNER

Ihr leistungsstarker Fach-Distributor für Hard- und Software

NAM GmbH
Kieler Straße 13
6000 Frankfurt/M 80

Tel. 069/307 61 61
Fax 069/307 78 23

Firma
Computech GmbH
Frau G. Fink
Radarthalgürtel 306–308
5000 Köln 51

Kunden-Nr. 34/556/D

Rechnung

Frankfurt 2. Juli 19 ...

Ihre Bestellung vom 23. Juni 19 ... Best. Nr. ST/990123-2
Versandart: durch Post

Anzahl	Artikel-Nr.	Artikel	Einzelpreis DM	Betrag DM
1	Q302	105MB Quantum Festplatte	1160,00	1160,00
2	Q303	210MB Quantum Festplatte	1850,00	3700,00
8	FX2	4MB SIMM für Mac II FX	375,00	3000,00
				7860,00
		MwSt. 15%		1179,00
				9039,00

Beanstandungen nur innerhalb 8 Tagen

EXPLANATIONS AND EXERCISES

EXERCISE 5.7
Here are some more verbs with *haben* and *sein*.
Translate the following sentences into English:

a *Wir haben die Rechnung durchgefaxt.*
b *Wir sind schon voll belegt.*
c *Ich habe die Rechnung erhalten.*
d *Sie hat den Kundenrabatt nicht abgezogen.*
e *Wir haben das übersehen.*
f *Wir haben drei Prozent Rabatt vereinbart.*

EXERCISE 5.8
Listen to dialogue 5.3. Are the following statements *richtig* or *falsch*?

a *Die Lieferbedingungen stimmen nicht.*
b *Der Rechnungsbetrag stimmt nicht.*
c *Die Lieferscheine fehlen.*
d *Sie hat die Rechnung am 2.7. erhalten.*
e *Wir hatten fünf Prozent Mengenrabatt vereinbart.*

EXERCISE 5.9
Your accounts department has asked you for help with the invoice from NAM (opposite). They urgently need the following information:

a order number
b date of the order
c total, excluding VAT
d VAT (per cent)
e agreed discounts (per cent)

● PRODUCTION PROBLEMS ●

KEY WORDS AND PHRASES

leider müssen wir Ihnen mitteilen	we are sorry to inform you
die Festplatte (-n)	hard disk
fristgerecht	on the agreed date
bedingt durch	caused by/due to
der Zulieferer (-)	supplier
. . . werden versandbereit sein	. . . will be ready for dispatch
es tut uns leid, Ihnen Unannehmlichkeiten verursacht zu haben	we apologize for any inconvenience we may have caused you
wir danken Ihnen für Ihr Verständnis in dieser Angelegenheit	we thank you for your understanding in this matter

5.4 🎧 YOUR ORDER OF ...

NAM PARTNER

NAM GmbH
Kieler Straße 13
6000 Frankfurt/M 80

*Ihr leistungsstarker
Fach-Distributor für
Hard- und Software*

Tel. 069/307 61 61
Fax 069/307 78 23

Herrn Dr. W. Schreiber
Geschäftsführer
Computech GmbH
Radarthalgürtel 306–308
5000 Köln 51

Ihre Bestellung vom 13.4.19 ...   22.4.19 ...

Sehr geehrter Herr Dr. Schreiber,

leider müssen wir Ihnen mitteilen, daß wir die Festplatten IISI nicht fristgerecht liefern können. Wir haben zur Zeit Produktionsschwierigkeiten, bedingt durch unsere Zulieferer.

Die Festplatten werden innerhalb der nächsten 2–3 Wochen versandbereit sein.

Es tut uns leid, Ihnen Unannehmlichkeiten verursacht zu haben. Wir danken Ihnen für Ihr Verständnis in dieser Angelegenheit.

Mit freundlichen Grüßen

F. Huber
Produktionsleiter

EXPLANATIONS AND EXERCISES

Word order

Note that the (finite) verb goes to the end in the *daß* sentence:

*Es tut uns leid, **daß** wir Produktionsschwierigkeiten **haben**.*
*Ich glaube, **daß** der Rechnungsbetrag nicht **stimmt**.*
*Wir müssen Ihnen mitteilen, **daß** wir nicht fristgerecht liefern **können**.*

EXERCISE 5.10
Translate the following negative opening statements:

a We are sorry to inform you that the products are not in stock.
b We are sorry to inform you that the quantity delivered is incorrect.
c We are sorry to inform you that we are already fully booked.

EXERCISE 5.11
Brief your English boss on the main points of the letter from NAM.

EXERCISE 5.12
Find German equivalents in the letter from NAM on page 87 for the following phrases:

a *Es tut uns leid, Ihnen mitteilen zu müssen* . . .
b *Die Festplatten sind nicht vorrätig.*
c *Wir haben im Moment Schwierigkeiten mit der Produktion.*

LETTER BEGINNINGS

Ich danke Ihnen für Ihr Schreiben vom . . .
Thank you for your letter of . . .

Wir freuen uns, Ihnen mitteilen zu können, daß . . .
We are pleased to inform you that . . .

— *Leider sind wir nicht in der Lage . . .*
Unfortunately we are not in a position . . .

Bezugnehmend auf Ihr Schreiben vom . . .
With reference to your letter of . . .

Ich beziehe mich auf unser Telefonat vom . . .
With reference to our telephone conversation of . . .

● CANCELLATION OF AN ORDER ●

KEY WORDS AND PHRASES

die Produktionsschwierigkeiten (pl.)	production problems
Sie müssen sich gedulden	you'll have to be patient
akzeptabel	acceptable
die Bestellung annullieren	cancel the order
früher geht's nicht	we can't manage any earlier
wir müssen uns einen anderen Lieferanten suchen	we'll have to find a different supplier

Cancellation of an order

5.5 WE HAVE TO CANCEL THE ORDER

DR. SCHREIBER Herr Huber, ich habe gerade Ihren Brief erhalten. Sie haben Produktionsschwierigkeiten mit den Festplatten?

HERR HUBER Ja, Sie müssen sich leider noch drei bis vier Wochen mit der Lieferung gedulden.

DR. SCHREIBER Drei bis vier Wochen! Aber in Ihrem Brief schreiben Sie zwei bis drei Wochen.

HERR HUBER Tut mir leid, das ist mein Fehler, früher geht's nicht.

DR. SCHREIBER Also, das ist nicht akzeptabel, Herr Huber. Dann müssen wir die Bestellung annullieren und uns einen anderen Lieferanten suchen.

EXPLANATIONS AND EXERCISES

EXERCISE 5.13
Listen to dialogue 5.5 and decide which route in the flow chart represents the conversation correctly.

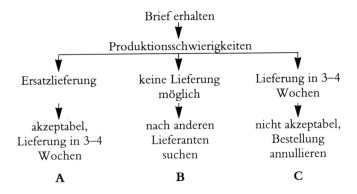

EXERCISE 5.14

Herr Huber is ringing you to enquire about an overdue delivery. Your task is to stall him for another week.

HERR HUBER	Wir haben die Lieferung der Modems vom 3. April noch nicht erhalten.
SIE	(Say you are having production problems with the modems at the moment.)
HERR HUBER	Wann können Sie liefern?
SIE	(Tell him you are sorry, but he'll have to be patient for another week.)
HERR HUBER	Gut, also dann in einer Woche.
SIE	(Thank him for his understanding.)

WORTH KNOWING

Form of the business letter
Although secretarial colleges in German-speaking countries usually insist that there is only one correct form of business letter, in practice you'll find that the form is variable. Certain general rules, however, are adhered to with variations in detail. All companies use headed paper including address, telephone and fax numbers with pre-printed slots for date and reference initials. Unlike in English-speaking countries, the headed stationery also contains company banking details.

Address
You'll have noticed that in German addresses the house number follows the street, and the postcode precedes the town with a number for the district following it:

Herrn Holger Müller *Frau Gertrude Meyer*
Mühlenstraße 32 *Johannisburger Str. 26*

5090 Leverkusen 1 *0-6900 Jena*

After unification there was a need to distinguish between East and West German towns with the same postcode. Thus some German addresses displayed the prefix O for *Ost* or W for *West* in front of the postcode. However, on 1 July 1993 the German *Bundespost* introduces a new, unified system of postcodes. In future there will be five digits instead of four. To make sure that you use the right postcodes on your letters you can ring up the *Deutsche Bundespost* and ask them to send you a booklet with the new codes (*ein Verzeichnis der Postleitzahlen*).

If you are sending a letter from abroad you need to put a D for *Deutschland* in front of the postcode.

Special instructions on your letter could include:

Einschreiben	registered mail
Luftpost	air mail
Persönlich	personal
Eilt	urgent
Vertraulich	private and confidential

Salutation
Sehr geehrte Damen und Herren is a rather formal salutation and equivalent to 'Dear Sir/Madam'. When a more personal relationship has been established, it is usual to address a person by his or her name and/or title: *Sehr geehrte Frau Unruh* or *Sehr geehrter Herr Dr. Schreiber*. Only when you know someone well may you start using *Liebe Frau Unruh* or *Lieber Herr Krüger*.

Close
The standard complimentary close is almost always *Mit freundlichen Grüßen*, which is equivalent to 'Yours sincerely'. If the letter contains any enclosures you will find the word *Anlagen* below the signature. Should you wish to send copies of your letter to other people in the organization, you need to write *Verteiler* at the bottom of the letter and list the names and/or departments you wish your letter to be sent to.

SELF-ASSESSMENT

Tick the following categories for your self-assessment guide:

	from memory (A)	with some reference to the text (B)	with full support (C)
I can understand and check the details of an acknowledgement of order			
I can query incorrect details over the phone			
I can read and write a simple hotel reservation and book a room by phone			
I can understand and query the details on an invoice			
I can understand the gist of a simple business letter and relay that information			
I can cancel and stall an order on the phone			

This unit is particularly difficult so don't worry if there are a few Bs this time.

6 WINING AND DINING

● ABOUT UNIT 6 ●

In this unit you'll follow up an invitation to lunch, study the menu and order a three-course meal in German. You'll learn how to thank your hosts for their hospitality, return the invitation and say your goodbyes.

● AN INVITATION ●

KEY WORDS AND PHRASES

dann haben wir ja alles Geschäftliche besprochen	so that's the business side dealt with
jetzt	now
zum Mittagessen einladen	to invite to lunch
sehr gern, vielen Dank	I'd love to, thank you
vorschlagen	to suggest
'Bärenwirt'	*name of the restaurant*
um die Ecke	round the corner
das Essen (-)	food, meal
einverstanden	that's fine with me
kann ich meine Tasche im Büro lassen?	can I leave my briefcase in the office?
ja, natürlich, lassen Sie ruhig alles hier	yes, of course, you can leave everything here

An invitation

6.1 MAY I INVITE YOU TO LUNCH?

HERR KLEIN . . . so, dann haben wir ja alles Geschäftliche besprochen, Frau Seifert. Darf ich Sie jetzt zum Mittagessen einladen?

FRAU SEIFERT Sehr gern, vielen Dank.

HERR KLEIN Ich schlage vor, wir gehen zum Bärenwirt, das ist gleich um die Ecke, und das Essen ist wirklich sehr gut da.

FRAU SEIFERT Einverstanden. Kann ich meine Tasche hier im Büro lassen?

HERR KLEIN Ja, natürlich, lassen Sie ruhig alles hier.

EXPLANATIONS AND EXERCISES

Inviting people

When inviting someone, use *zur* (*zu der*) with feminine nouns and *zum* (*zu dem*) with masculine and neuter nouns:

Ich möchte Sie	**zur** *Party* (f.)	*einladen.*
Darf ich Sie	**zum** *Kaffee* (m.)	*einladen?*
Darf ich Sie	**zum** *Essen* (n.)	*einladen?*

However, if you are inviting someone to a place, such as the theatre, opera or restaurant you use *ins* (*in das*) with neuter nouns, *in die* with feminine and *in den* with masculine nouns:

*Darf ich Sie **ins** Theater einladen?*
*Darf ich Sie **in die** Oper einladen?*
*Darf ich Sie **ins** Restaurant Melle einladen?*
*Darf ich Sie **in den** Thüringer Hof einladen?*

EXERCISE 6.1
Invite a business colleague:

a for coffee
b to the restaurant Käfer
c to the theatre
d for lunch

EXERCISE 6.2
Herr Klein has invited you for lunch and asks you to suggest a suitable restaurant.

HERR KLEIN	Können Sie ein Restaurant empfehlen?
SIE	(Suggest the Bärenwirt. Say the food is really good there.)
HERR KLEIN	Können wir zu Fuß gehen?
SIE	(Say yes, it's just round the corner.)

• AT THE RESTAURANT (1) •

KEY WORDS AND PHRASES

die Speisekarte (-n)	menu
darf ich Ihnen schon etwas zu Trinken bringen?	would you like a drink beforehand?
das Mineralwasser (-)	mineral water
ein kleines Pils	a small pilsner (lager)
haben Sie schon gewählt?	are you ready to order?
der Salatteller (-)	a mixed salad
als Vorspeise	as a starter
der Rheinische Sauerbraten (-)	braised beef marinated in vinegar, herbs and raisins
die Gemüsesuppe (-n)	vegetable soup
der Kalbsbraten (-)	roast veal
die Pommes Frites (pl.)	chips

At the restaurant (1)

6.2 THE MENU, PLEASE

HERR KLEIN Die Speisekarte, bitte.
OBER Gern, einen Moment, bitte. (*hands over the menu*) Hier, bitte schön, die Speisekarte. Darf ich Ihnen schon etwas zu Trinken bringen?
FRAU SEIFERT Ich hätte gern ein Mineralwasser.
HERR KLEIN Und ich nehme ein kleines Pils.
OBER Ein Mineralwasser und ein kleines Pils. Kommt sofort . . .

6.3 🎧 HAVE YOU CHOSEN?

OBER	Haben Sie schon gewählt?
FRAU SEIFERT	Ja, ich hätte gern einen kleinen Salatteller als Vorspeise und dann den Rheinischen Sauerbraten.
OBER	Und der Herr?
HERR KLEIN	Für mich eine Gemüsesuppe, bitte, und einmal Kalbsbraten mit Pommes Frites.
OBER	Ja, gern.

• AT THE RESTAURANT (2) •

KEY WORDS AND PHRASES

hat es Ihnen geschmeckt?	did you enjoy the meal?
der Nachtisch (-e)	dessert
die Nachspeise (-n)	dessert
reichhaltig	substantial (meal)
Apfelstrudel mit Sahne	apple strudel with cream
der Kaffee (-s)	coffee
wir möchten zahlen, bitte	we'd like the bill, please
getrennt oder zusammen?	(are you paying) separately or together?
stimmt so	that's all right
das nächste Mal sind Sie dann mein Gast	next time you'll be my guest

At the restaurant (2)

6.4 DID YOU ENJOY THE MEAL?

OBER	Hat es Ihnen geschmeckt?
FRAU SEIFERT	Ausgezeichnet, vielen Dank.
OBER	Darf ich Ihnen noch einen Nachtisch bringen?
FRAU SEIFERT	Für mich nicht, danke, das Essen war so reichhaltig.
OBER	Und für Sie?
HERR KLEIN	Ich nehme einen Apfelstrudel mit Sahne, bitte. Vielleicht einen Kaffee, Frau Seifert?
FRAU SEIFERT	Ja, gern.
HERR KLEIN	Und zwei Kaffee, bitte.
OBER	Kommt sofort.

6.5 THE BILL, PLEASE!

HERR KLEIN	Herr Ober, wir möchten zahlen, bitte.
OBER	Geht das getrennt oder zusammen?
HERR KLEIN	Zusammen, bitte.
OBER	. . . und zwei Kaffee, ein Mineralwasser und zwei kleine Pils . . . das macht 49,95 DM.
HERR KLEIN	Fünfzig, fünfundfünfzig – stimmt so.
OBER	Vielen Dank auch.
FRAU SEIFERT	Ich bedanke mich auch, Herr Klein; das nächste Mal sind Sie dann mein Gast.

EXPLANATIONS AND EXERCISES

Ordering

To ask for the menu you can say: *die Speisekarte, bitte* or, if you wish to order drinks, *die Getränkekarte, bitte* or, more specific, *die Weinkarte, bitte*. If you ask for *das Menü, bitte* you'll get the fixed-price set meal of the day! If the choice on the *Speisekarte* is too daunting, ask the waiter for a recommendation: *Was können Sie empfehlen?*

When it's your turn to order, the waiter might ask: . . . *und für Sie?* . . . and for you? Start by saying: *Für mich bitte* . . . , then name the dish; or you can use one of the phrases you already know: *Ich hätte gern* . . . or *ich möchte* . . . or *ich nehme* . . .

Ich hätte gern . . .	das/ein	*Rumpsteak.*
Ich möchte . . .	die/eine	*Gemüsesuppe.*
Ich nehme . . .	den/einen	*Sauerbraten.*

If the dish or drink you order is a masculine word, you use *einen* or *den*. To say what you would like for a particular course, use: *als Vorspeise* (as a starter); or *als Hauptgang* (as a main course), but watch out for the different word order:

Als Vorspeise	*hätte ich gern* . . .	*die/eine Gemüsesuppe.*
Als Hauptgang	*möchte ich* . . .	*das/ein Rumpsteak.*
Als Nachspeise	*nehme ich* . . .	*den/einen Apfelstrudel.*

EXERCISE 6.3
You and your colleague have studied the menu opposite and are now ready to order. Look up any unfamiliar words and their gender in the word list at the back, then complete the order.

SIE   Als Vorspeise hätte ich gern ____ Salat Niçoise, dann ____ Kalbsbraten, und als Nachspeise nehme ich ____ Sachertorte.

KOLLEGE Also ich möchte ____ Gemüsesuppe, dann ____ Rheinischen Sauerbraten, und als Nachspeise nehme ich ____ Obstsalat.

EXERCISE 6.4
Listen to dialogue 6.6 (tape only) and find out what this rather difficult customer finally decides to order. Tick the dishes on the menu opposite.

Speisekarte

Vorspeisen

Gulaschsuppe	DM 5,80
Zwiebelsuppe	DM 5,60
Gemüsesuppe	DM 4,50
Nudelsuppe	DM 4,50
Kraftbrühe	DM 3,80
Schinkenplatte	DM 11,20
Salat Niçoise	DM 12,00
Heringstopf	DM 9,60

Hauptgerichte

Wiener Schitzel m. Pommes Frites, Salat	DM 15,80
Kalbsbraten m. Röstkartoffeln, Gemüse	DM 14,90
Rhein. Sauerbraten m. Klößen, Rotkraut	DM 13,90
Lammkotelett m. Röstkartoffeln, Salat	DM 17,80
Heilbuttsteak in Rahmsauce, Reis	DM 17,90
Rotbarschfilet m. Sauce Holland., Reis	DM 16,00
Forelle blau m. Salzkartoffeln, Salat	DM 18,20

Nachspeisen

Apfelstrudel	DM 5,50
Himbeertorte	DM 6,80
Sachertorte	DM 6,80
Eisbecher m. Früchten	DM 7,00
Heiße Liebe (Vanilleeis m. heißen Himbeeren)	DM 6,50
Obstsalat	DM 5,80

EXERCISE 6.5

Sie or *Ihnen*?

a Darf ich _____ zum Essen einladen?
b Kann ich _____ schon etwas zu Trinken bringen?
c Ich kann _____ den Sauerbraten empfehlen.
d Hat es _____ geschmeckt?

EXERCISE 6.6

Listen to dialogue 6.4 again, then reconstruct it below by matching up the sentences from both columns.

Hat es Ihnen	einen Nachtisch bringen?
Ausgezeichnet,	Sie?
Darf ich Ihnen noch	geschmeckt?
Für mich nicht,	einen Kaffee, Frau Seifert?
Und für	einen Apfelstrudel mit Sahne, bitte.
Ich nehme	danke, das Essen war so reichhaltig.
Vielleicht	vielen Dank.

EXERCISE 6.7
You've finished your meal and want to pay:

OBER	Hat es Ihnen geschmeckt?
SIE	(Say you found it excellent, and ask for the bill.)
OBER	Geht das getrennt oder zusammen?
SIE	(Together, please.)
OBER	Das macht 55,30 DM zusammen, bitte.
SIE	(You hand over 60 marks and say that's fine.)

● THANK YOU AND GOODBYE ●

KEY WORDS AND PHRASES

verabschieden	to say goodbye
die Gastfreundschaft (-en)	hospitality
ich melde mich dann bei Ihnen	I'll get in touch with you
ich freue mich auf die Zusammenarbeit mit Ihrer Firma	I look forward to working with your company
gute Heimreise	have a good journey back

Thank you and goodbye

6.7 THANK YOU FOR YOUR HOSPITALITY

FRAU SEIFERT	So, ich muß mich leider jetzt verabschieden, Herr Klein. Ich bedanke mich für Ihre Gastfreundschaft. Ich melde mich dann bei Ihnen mit den Lieferterminen.
HERR KLEIN	In Ordnung, und ich bedanke mich für Ihren Besuch und freue mich auf die Zusammenarbeit mit Ihrer Firma.
FRAU SEIFERT	Vielen Dank. Auf Wiedersehen.
HERR KLEIN	Auf Wiedersehen und gute Heimreise.

EXPLANATIONS AND EXERCISES

Thanking people
To thank someone for hospitality you can say: *Ich bedanke mich für Ihre Gastfreundschaft*, and offer to reciprocate next time round: *Das nächste Mal sind Sie mein Gast.* You may wish to extend an invitation for a visit: *Darf ich Sie zu einem Besuch nach . . . einladen?*

Goodbyes
Before the proverbial *auf Wiedersehen*, accompanied by a handshake, you may say: *Vielen Dank für Ihren Besuch* or *Ich bedanke mich für Ihren Besuch.* To say that you'll be in touch you simply use: *Ich melde mich dann bei Ihnen* or a variation of this phrase as above: *Ich melde mich dann bei Ihnen mit den Lieferterminen.*

And to wish your guest a safe journey home: *Gute Heimreise!* or *Ich wünsche Ihnen eine gute Heimreise!* Among people who know each other well, you may hear the more colloquial *Tschüs* for goodbye.

More about verbs
When you look up words such as *verabschieden, bedanken, melden, freuen* (reflexive verbs) you'll notice the entry in the word list is *sich verabschieden, sich melden*, etc. This indicates that you need to add a *mich* in the first person:

ich verabschiede mich; ich bedanke mich; ich melde mich; ich freue mich.

EXERCISE 6.8
Translate the following sentences into German.

a Thank you for your hospitality (lit. I thank you . . .).
b I look forward to working with you.
c I'll get in touch with you next week.
d I'm afraid I'll have to say goodbye now.

WORTH KNOWING

Calling the waiter or waitress
Calling the waiter is easy. Just say *Herr Ober!* In a pub you may hear *Herr Wirt* if the landlord himself is working behind the bar. It used to be customary to call the waitress *Fräulein*, but today waitresses increasingly resent this form of address, which was originally used for unmarried women. It is safer, therefore, just to say *Entschuldigung* or indicate with your hand that you want her attention.

Breakfast
Most hotels serve continental breakfast consisting of tea or coffee, a selection of cereals, fruit juices, a variety of different breads and rolls, butter and jam. In addition, you'll normally find sliced cheese and a selection of cold meats. In most hotels, guests help themselves from a buffet. Breakfast tends to be included in the price of your room, but it's safer to check. Just ask: *Ist das mit Frühstück?*

Lunch and dinner
If you go to a restaurant for a meal and want the menu, ask for *die Karte* or *die Speisekarte*. If you can't make out what the various dishes are, play safe and ask for the set meal called *das Gedeck* or *das Menü*. It is often the best buy. You will hear the waiter or waitress use *einmal, zweimal*, etc. as they list your order. You can also use *einmal, zweimal* when ordering, for example: *einmal Menü 2 und zweimal Rheinischer Sauerbraten, bitte*. Restaurant charges normally include service, but it's common to add a tip of about ten per cent to the bill. You can either round up the amount and say *stimmt so* or leave the tip and say *das ist für Sie*.

Guten Appetit
It is a common gesture to wish each other *guten Appetit* (enjoy your meal) before the meal, whether you are in a restaurant or eating with a family. If you are invited for a meal at a colleague's house, German etiquette stipulates that you take your cue to start the meal from the lady of the house.

Drinks

The variety of German wines is almost impossible to describe. The *Riesling* and *Müller-Thurgau* are the two great grapes of Germany which produce nearly all the best German wines. But bear in mind the different quality designations. They range from cheap table wines (*Landwein* and *Deutscher Tafelwein*) to quality wines (*Qualitätswein*) and quality wines with distinction (*Qualitätswein mit Prädikat*) such as *Kabinett*, *Spätlese*, *Auslese* and *Beerenauslese* wines in ascending order of quality and price.

Germany is also well known for its beer, and the choice is vast. It is preferable to buy draught (*vom Faß*) rather than by the bottle (*eine Flasche*), which usually doesn't taste as good and is more expensive. Whether you are in a pub or a restaurant you would normally not get a drink from the

bar but sit down and wait to be served. You're not expected to pay immediately, instead the waiter notes down the drink on your beer mat for payment before you leave. Most pubs stay open until midnight or one o'clock in the morning.

Ruhetag
Most restaurants are closed for one day of the week, usually indicated by a sign *Ruhetag* (lit. rest day) on the door.

SELF-ASSESSMENT

Tick the following categories for your self-assessment:

	from memory (A)	with some reference to the text (B)	with full support (C)
I can accept a lunch invitation and invite someone for a meal myself			
I can recommend a restaurant			
I can read a simple menu and place an order for food and drink			
I can understand the gist of someone else's order			
I can request the bill and give a tip			
I can return an invitation and thank my host for his/her hospitality			

If you are satisfied with your performance in this unit, you may find it useful to go back over past assessments and revise where necessary. We hope you've enjoyed the course and that you now feel able to 'get by' in business German.

REFERENCE SECTION

● PRONUNCIATION ●

German pronunciation isn't really difficult. The best way to get it right is to listen carefully to the cassettes and copy what you hear as closely as possible. This pronunciation guide is recorded at the beginning of the second cassette with pauses for you to repeat the words. Go through it as often as you like until you feel really confident

VOWELS

Vowels can be long or short. Double vowels are long, as in *Tee* or *Kaffee*. And vowels are long before an *h*, as in *gehen*. Before a double consonant they are short, as in *Herr* or *Zimmer*.

a	long	*Sahne, haben*	o	long	*groß, oder*
	short	*danke, Angebot*		short	*kommen, kostet*
e	long	*gehen, nehmen*	u	long	*gut, Dusche*
	short	*gern, Herr*		short	*zum, und*
i	long	*Ihnen, Kilo*			
	short	*bitte, ist*			

VOWELS WITH *UMLAUTS*

These have no English equivalents. Listen to the cassette and copy the pronunciation as closely as you can.

ä	long	*fährt, ungefähr*	ü	long	*für, Menü*
	short	*ärgerlich, Äpfel*		short	*fünf, Stück*
ö	long	*schön, hören*			
	short	*möchte, können*			

VOWEL COMBINATIONS

au	like 'ow' in 'how'	*Frau, aus*
ai *ei* }	like 'y' in 'my'	*Mai* *Wein*
ie	like 'ee' in 'tree'	*die, hier*
äu *eu* }	like 'oy' in 'toy'	*läuft, äußerst* *Deutsch, neu*

CONSONANTS

Most sound similar to English, but there are some points to notice.

ch	after *a, o, u* and *au* like 'ch' in the Scottish 'loch'	*macht, noch auch, Kuchen*
	otherwise like 'h' in huge	*ich, rechts*
chs	like 'x' in 'sex'	*sechs*
d	at the end of a word, like 't'	*bald*
-ig	at the end of a word, usually as in *ich*	*zwanzig*
j	like 'y' in 'you'	*ja, Jahr*
r	rolled from the back of the throat	*Rabatt, rechts*
sch	like 'sh' in 'shop'	*schicken, Dusche*
sp	at the beginning of a word, 'shp'	*sprechen*
st	at the beginning of a word, 'sht'	*Stück, Straße*
v	like 'f' in 'for'	*vier, von*
w	like 'v' in 'vine'	*weit, auf Wiedersehen*
z	like 'ts' in 'cats'	*zehn, zu*

• DAYS OF THE WEEK •

Sonntag	Sunday	*Donnerstag*	Thursday
Montag	Monday	*Freitag*	Friday
Dienstag	Tuesday	*Samstag* or	Saturday
Mittwoch	Wednesday	*Sonnabend*	

• MONTHS OF THE YEAR •

Januar	January	*Juli*	July
Februar	February	*August*	August
März	March	*September*	September
April	April	*Oktober*	October
Mai	May	*November*	November
Juni	June	*Dezember*	December

• COUNTRIES •

Österreich	Austria	*Nordirland*	Northern Ireland
Belgien	Belgium		
Bulgarien	Bulgaria	*Norwegen*	Norway
Kanada	Canada	*Polen*	Poland
China	China	*Portugal*	Portugal
Tschechoslowakei (f)	Czechoslovakia	*Rumänien*	Romania
Dänemark	Denmark	*Rußland*	Russia
Irland	Eire	*Schottland*	Scotland
Finnland	Finland	*Spanien*	Spain
Frankreich	France	*Schweiz (f)*	Switzerland
Großbritannien	Great Britain	*Türkei (f)*	Turkey
Griechenland	Greece	*Vereinigtes Königreich*	United Kingdom
Ungarn	Hungary		
Italien	Italy	*die Vereinigten Staaten von Amerika*	USA
Japan	Japan		
Luxemburg	Luxembourg		
Holland	Netherlands	*Wales*	Wales

KEY TO EXERCISES

● UNIT 1 ●

1.1 **a** fünfunddreißig **b** einundvierzig **c** neunundfünfzig **d** achtundachtzig **e** sechsundneunzig

1.2 **a** Wo ist die Firma Häussler? **b** Wo ist der Hauptausgang? **c** Wo ist das Hotel zum goldenen Löwen?

1.3 **a** Wie komme ich zum Hauptbahnhof? **b** Wie komme ich zur S-Bahn? **c** Wie komme ich zur Messe? **d** Wie komme ich nach Frankfurt?

1.4 Gehen Sie geradeaus, dann nehmen Sie die nächste rechts, gehen Sie bis zur Lindenstraße. Das Hotel ist gegenüber dem Bahnhof.

1.5 fährt (die Straßenbahn), ist (die Haltestelle), ist (das), entschuldigen (Sie), möchte (ich), ist (das/welche Zone), ist (das), kostet (das), macht (das), fährt (der Zug).

1.6 Wie weit ist es zum Flughafen, bitte?
Entschuldigen Sie bitte, wie komme ich zur Messe?

1.7
HERR WINKLER	Entschuldigung, wo fährt die Straßenbahn zur Messe ab, bitte?
PASSANT	Hier geradeaus, die Haltestelle ist gegenüber dem Theater.
HERR WINKLER	Ist das weit von hier?
PASSANT	Nein, zwei Minuten zu Fuß.
HERR WINKLER	Danke schön.

1.8 **1**c **2**d **3**a

1.9 See the map opposite above.

● UNIT 2 ●

2.1 **1**c **2**f **3**a **4**d **5**b **6**e

2.2 Schulte   Roth

2.3 Check on page 27 in unit 2.

2.4 2 – 8 – 4 – 7 – 1 – 5 –3/6

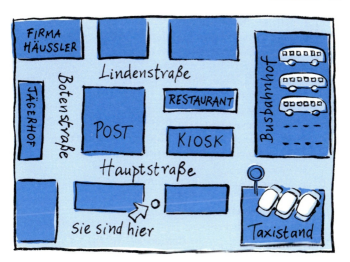

2.5 Guten Tag, mein Name ist . . . Ich möchte einen Termin mit Frau Breuer vereinbaren.
Mein Name ist . . .
Ja, das geht. Vielen Dank. Auf Wiederhören.
2.6 eine, dem, dem
2.7 Gut danke, und Ihnen?
Ja danke, kein Problem.
Ja bitte (schwarz ohne/mit Zucker) or (mit Milch und Zucker).
2.8 Unruh, Sassen & Co., Einkaufsleiterin, Dienstag/Mittwoch nachmittag, Tel. 0711-23 76 91
Bernd Schmidt, Peters, Montag 15.00 Uhr, Tel. 040-66 21 21

● UNIT 3 ●

3.1 mache, machst, macht, machen, macht, machen, machen
3.2 ist, bin, habe, ist, sind
3.3 Sassen & Co., Frau Unruh, purchasing department, send catalogue and price list
3.4 For answers, refer to dialogue 3.2 on your tape.

3.5   **a** Ich möchte bitte (mit) Herrn Kaufmann sprechen.
     b Leider muß ich den Termin absagen.
     c Darf ich Sie morgen zurückrufen?
     d Wann kann ich ihn erreichen?

3.6   Mein, Ihrem, Ihren, Ihre, Ihr, Ihre, Ihre

3.7   Correct point: 2

3.8   **a** Was/Wieviel kostet eine Fahrkarte nach Stuttgart?
     b Was/Wieviel kostet ein Taxi zum Hauptbahnhof?
     c Was/Wieviel kosten die Entsafter?
     d Was/Wieviel kostet der Espresso-Automat?

3.9   **1**c   **2**a   **3**d

3.10 **a** Ich bedanke mich für Ihren Auftrag.
      b Ich muß mit unserem Lager sprechen.

3.11 Ich möchte 30 Kaffeeautomaten, Kenia 2000, zum 1. Dezember bestellen.
Ich möchte 15 Espresso-Automaten, Verona V20, für Woche 21 bestellen.

3.12 WY-33 709, 40 cartons Pizza Romana, 25 cartons quiche lorraine, delivery week 32.

● UNIT 4 ●

4.1   **a** neuen **b** defekten **c** neue

4.2   **a** Unsere Kunden beanstanden, daß die Modems gefährlich sind.
     b Unsere Kunden beanstanden, daß die neuen Modelle zu teuer sind.
     c Unsere Kunden beanstanden, daß die Kaffeeautomaten nicht funktionieren.

4.3   **b** Überprüfen Sie das doch bitte sofort!
     c Schicken Sie uns doch bitte eine neue Preisliste!
     d Rufen Sie doch bitte sobald wie möglich zurück!

4.4   Problem mit neuen Modems, Modems überhitzen leicht, Modelle WS 300, V22 und V23, mit Fertigungsingenieur sprechen, sobald wie möglich zurückrufen

4.5   **a** Was machen wir mit den defekten Maschinen?
     b Wann erhalten wir die Ersatzlieferung?
     c Wie schicken Sie die neuen Maschinen?

4.6 das Problem lösen, die Lieferung erhalten, die defekten Modems ersetzen
4.7
   a Das ist die Bestellung vom 10. Juni.
   b Das ist die Rechnung vom 7. Mai.
   c Das ist die Lieferung vom 13. Dezember.
4.8
   a Wir brauchen die Lieferung spätestens am Dienstag, den 28. März.
   b Wir brauchen den Bericht am Mittwoch.
   c Wir brauchen die Maschinen bis zum 21. April.
4.9 Computech in Köln – Ersatzlieferung noch nicht erhalten. Bestellung vom 4. Oktober – Modems V22 und V23. Ersatzlieferung schicken – Modems vorrätig. Lieferung spätestens bis Freitag.
4.10 **b** and **e**
4.11 **c**
4.12 Die Lieferung ist zu spät angekommen. Sie haben uns die falsche Menge geschickt. Wir haben die Zahlungen noch nicht erhalten.
Ich habe mit dem Chef gesprochen. Sie haben uns eine Ersatzlieferung geschickt. Sie haben die Rechnung beglichen. Wir haben die Probleme gelöst.
4.13
   a Ich habe gute Nachrichten für Sie, Frau Fink.
   b Ich habe die überfälligen Zahlungen am 12. Januar auf Ihr Konto überwiesen.

• UNIT 5 •

5.1
   a Stellen Sie das Gespräch durch.
   b Ich hole Sie vom Flughafen ab.
   c Ich faxe Ihnen die Tagesordnung durch.
   d Ich rufe Sie später zurück.
5.2 in, für, bei, von, nach
5.3
   a yes, no
   b agreed terms: drei Prozent Mengenrabatt
stated on fax: drei Prozent Skonto bei Zahlung innerhalb von 10 Tagen nach Rechnungsdatum.
   c yes, no, yes
5.4 **c**

5.5 **a** Doppelzimmer mit Bad/WC **b** 158 DM
5.6 Suggested answer:

Your name
and address

_____

Hotel Wiese
Bahnhofstraße 3
D/W-7000 Stuttgart 1

London, 1.2.19...

Sehr geehrte Damen und Herren,

Zimmerreservierung

bitte reservieren Sie ein Einzelzimmer mit Bad/WC für zwei Nächte vom 12.–14. Februar, Adresse obenstehend.

Bitte bestätigen Sie die Buchung so bald wie möglich.

Mit freundlichen Grüßen,

5.7 **a** We have faxed through the invoice.
   b We are already fully booked.
   c I have received the invoice.
   d She has not deducted the customer discount.
   e It's an oversight on our part.
   f We agreed a discount of three per cent.
5.8 **a** falsch **b** richtig **c** falsch **d** falsch **e** richtig
5.9 **a** ST/990123-2 **b** 23 June 19 . . . **c** 7860,00 DM
   d 15 per cent **e** five per cent
5.10 **a** Leider müssen wir Ihnen mitteilen, daß die Produkte nicht vorrätig sind.

b Leider müssen wir Ihnen mitteilen, daß die Liefermenge nicht stimmt.
   c Leider müssen wir Ihnen mitteilen, daß wir schon voll belegt sind.
5.11 Herr Huber apologizes that hard disks IISI cannot be delivered on the due date owing to production problems caused by NAM's suppliers. They will be dispatched within the next two or three weeks.
5.12 **a** Leider müssen wir Ihnen mitteilen . . .
   b Wir können die Festplatten nicht fristgerecht liefern.
   c Wir haben zur Zeit Produktionsschwierigkeiten.
5.13 C
5.14 Wir haben zur Zeit Produktionsprobleme mit den Modems.
Sie müssen sich leider noch eine Woche gedulden.
Ich danke Ihnen für Ihr Verständnis

● UNIT 6 ●

6.1 **a** Darf ich Sie zum Kaffee einladen?
   b Darf ich Sie ins Restaurant Käfer einladen?
   c Darf ich Sie ins Theater einladen?
   d Darf ich Sie zum Mittagessen einladen?
6.2 Ich schlage vor, wir gehen zum Bärenwirt. Das Essen ist wirklich gut da.
Ja, das ist gleich um die Ecke.
6.3 den/einen, den/einen, die/eine
die/eine, den/einen, den/einen
6.4 Kraftbrühe, Kalbsbraten, Obstsalat
6.5 **a** Sie **b** Ihnen **c** Ihnen **d** Ihnen
6.6 Check your answers against dialogue 6.4.
6.7 Ausgezeichnet (vielen Dank). Wir möchten zahlen, bitte.
Zusammen, bitte.
(Sechzig Mark), stimmt so.
6.8 **a** Ich bedanke mich für Ihre Gastfreundschaft.
   b Ich freue mich auf die Zusammenarbeit mit Ihnen.
   c Ich melde mich dann bei Ihnen nächste Woche.
   d Ich muß mich jetzt leider verabschieden.

WORD LIST

Abbreviations: (m.) masculine, (f.) feminine, (n.) neuter, (sing.) singular, (pl.) plural, (sep.) separable verbs, (lit.) literally, (col.) colloquial, (¨) umlaut in plural form. Plural forms of nouns are given in brackets.

The English meanings apply to the words as they are used in this book.

A

    ab 100 Stück for 100 or more
der *Abend* evening
    guten Abend good evening
    aber but
    abfahren (sep.) to leave from
    abholen (sep.) to pick up
    absagen (sep.) to cancel
    abziehen (sep.) to deduct
die *Adresse (-n)* address
die *Akte (-n)* file
    akzeptabel acceptable
    alles all, everything
    allgemein general
    im allgemeinen generally
die *allgemeinen Geschäftsbedingungen* terms of trade
    also . . . well then . . .
    am short for *an dem*
die *Ampel (-n)* traffic light
    an dem/der at the
    anbieten (sep.) to offer
    andere other
die *Anfrage (-n)* enquiry
das *Angebot (-e)* offer
die *Angelegenheit (-en)* matter
    angenehm pleasant, agreeable
    (sehr) angenehm pleased to meet you
der *Angestellte (-n)* employee (m.)
    ankommen (sep.) to arrive
die *Anlage (-n)* enclosure (correspondence)
    annullieren to cancel
    anrufen (sep.) to call (phone)
    anstatt instead of
die *Anzahl (-)* number
der *Apfel (¨)* apple
der *Apfelstrudel (-)* apple strudel
der *Apparat (-e)* phone
    bleiben sie am Apparat hold the line
    der Apparat ist im Moment besetzt the line is engaged at the moment
    arbeiten to work
    an die Arbeit! to work!
    ärgerlich annoying
    das ist wirklich sehr ärgerlich that's a real nuisance
der *Artikel (-)* item

die Artikel-Bezeichnung *(-en)* product description
die Artikel-Nummer *(-n)* product code
auch also, as well
der Auftrag *(¨e)* order
   im Auftrag p.p. (on behalf of)
die Auftragsbestätigung *(-en)* acknowledgement of order
ausgezeichnet splendid, excellent
äußerst extremely
ausführen (sep.) to carry out
der Ausländer *(-)* foreigner (m.)
die Ausländerin *(-nen)* foreigner (f.)
ausschließlich excluding
aussehen (sep.) to look
wie sieht es aus mit . . .? how about . . .?

B

die Bahn train
   mit der Bahn by train
der Bahnhof *(¨e)* railway station
bald soon
die Bank *(-en)* bank
der Beamte *(-n)* official
beanstanden to complain
die Beanstandung *(-en)* complaint
bedanken: sich bedanken to say thank you
   ich bedanke mich thank you
bedingt durch caused by/due to
die Bedingung *(-en)* term
begleichen to settle
   wir haben die Rechnung beglichen we have settled the invoice
beglichen see *begleichen*

bei (dem/der) at (the), near, for
   er arbeitet bei der Post he works for the post office
beim short for *bei dem*
bekommen to get
der Bericht *(-e)* report
berichtigen to amend
der Beruf *(-e)* job, profession
beschädigen to damage
besetzt engaged (phone)
besprechen to discuss
   wir haben alles besprochen we've discussed/dealt with everything
die Besprechung *(-en)* meeting
besprochen see *besprechen*
besser better
bestätigen to confirm
bestehen auf to insist on
bestellen to order
die Bestellmenge *(-n)* quantity ordered
die Bestellnummer *(-n)* order number
die Bestellung *(-en)* order
der Besuch *(-e)* visit
der Betrag *(¨e)* amount
betragen to amount to
beziehen auf: sich beziehen auf to refer to
das Bier *(-e)* beer
bin see *sein*
bis until, till
   bis zum/zur up to
bitte please
   bitte schön you're welcome
bitten to ask, to beg
bleiben to stay
brauchen to need
der Brief *(-e)* letter
die Buchhaltung *(-en)* accounting, accounts department

die *Buchmesse (-n)* book fair
buchstabieren to spell
die *Buchung (-en)* booking
das *Büro (-s)* office
der *Busbahnhof (¨-e)* bus depot

C

der *Chef (-s)* boss (m.)
die *Chefin (-nen)* boss (f.)

D

da drüben over there
danken to thank
danke schön/vielen Dank thank you/many thanks
dann then
darf see *dürfen*
das this, that, the
daß that
das *Datum (Daten)* date
dazwischenkommen (sep.) to come up/crop up
defekt faulty
dem, den, der the, this/that one
denken to think
  an was hatten Sie gedacht? what were you thinking of?
die the, that
die *Dienstleistung (-en)* service
diese, diesem, diesen, dieser this, these
DM=Deutsche Mark German Mark
das *Doppelzimmer (-)* double room
dringend urgent
durchfaxen (sep.) to fax through
durchgeben (sep.) to phone through
durchstellen (sep.) to put through (phone)
die *Durchwahl (-en)* direct line (phone)
dürfen to be allowed
  darf ich? may I?
die *Dusche (-n)* shower

E

die *Ecke (n)* corner
  um die Ecke round the corner
eilt! urgent!
ein, eine, einen, einer, einem a, one
einfach simple, simply
  einfache Fahrt single (ticket)
eingegangen see *eingehen*
eingehen (sep.) to arrive
  Ihre Zahlung ist eingegangen we have received your payment
der *Einkauf* shopping, also purchasing department
die *Einkaufsabteilung (-en)* purchasing department
der *Einkaufsleiter (-)* senior buyer (m.)
die *Einkaufsleiterin (-nen)* senior buyer (f.)
der *Einkaufspreis (-e)* cost price
einladen (sep.) to invite
einmal once, one (ticket)
  noch (ein)mal (once) again
einschließlich including
das *Einschreiben (-)* registered mail
eintragen: sich eintragen (sep.) to register
einverstanden! okay! agreed!
  (ich bin) einverstanden that's fine with me
der *Einzelpreis (-e)* unit price
das *Einzelzimmer (-)* single room
der *Eisbecher (-)* ice cream sundae

der Elektroartikel (-) electrical appliance
empfehlen to recommend
der Entsafter (-) juice extractor
die Entschuldigung (-en) excuse
   entschuldigen Sie bitte excuse me please
entwerten (einen Fahrschein) to date-stamp
er he
der Erfolg (-e) success
erfolgen to follow
   nach erfolgter Zahlung after payment has been effected/made
erhalten to receive
erinnern: sich erinnern to recall
erreichen to reach
die Ersatzlieferung (-en) replacement delivery
ersetzen to replace
erste first
   erster Klasse first class
erstens first of all
es it
der Espresso-Automat (-en) espresso machine
essen to eat
das Essen (-) food, meal
etwa about, approximately
etwas something

F

der Fahrausweis (-e) ticket
fahren to go, to drive
   der Zug fährt nach the train goes to
die Fahrkarte (-n) ticket
fährt see *fahren*
falls in case
falsch incorrect
faxen to fax

die Faxnachricht (-en) fax message
fehlen to be missing
der Fehler (-) mistake
der Fertigungsingenieur (-e) production engineer (m.)
die Festplatte (-n) hard disk
finden to find
   haben Sie . . . gefunden? did you find . . . ?
die Firma (Firmen) company
der Flughafen (¨) airport
folgen to follow
   die folgenden the following
die Forelle (-n) trout
   Forelle blau trout au bleu
die Frage (-n) query, question
fragen to ask
die Frau (-en) woman
   Frau . . . Mrs/Miss/Ms . . .
frei Haus carriage-free
freuen: sich freuen to be pleased
   es freut mich I'm pleased
sich freuen auf to look forward to
freundlich kind, friendly
   Mit freundlichen Grüßen yours sincerely
freut see *freuen*
fristgerecht on the agreed date
die Frucht (¨e) fruit
früh early
früher earlier
das Frühstück (-e) breakfast
funktionieren to work
   das Gerät funktioniert nicht the machine doesn't work
für for
der Fuß (¨e) foot
   zu Fuß on foot
   zwei Minuten zu Fuß two minutes' walk

G

der Gast (¨-e) guest (m.)
die Gastfreundschaft (-) hospitality
    geben to give
        es gibt there is/there are
das Gebiet (-e) area
    gedacht see denken
das Gedeck (-s) set menu
    gedulden: sich gedulden to be patient
    gefährlich dangerous
    gegenüber dem/der opposite the
    gehen to go
        das geht (nicht) that's (not) possible
        wie geht es Ihnen? how are you?
        es geht not too bad
das Gemüse (-) vegetables
die Gemüsesuppe (-n) vegetable soup
    genau exact
    gerade just
    geradeaus straight on
    gern geschehen you're welcome
    gesamt total
das Geschäft (-e) business
der Geschäftsführer (-) director (m.)
die Geschäftsführerin (-nen) director (f.)
der Geschäftspartner (-) business partner (m.)
die Geschäftspartnerin (-nen) business partner (f.)
der Geschenkartikel (-) giftware
    geschlossen closed
    geschmeckt see schmecken
das Gespräch see Telefongespräch
    gesprochen see sprechen
    gestern yesterday
die Getränkekarte (-n) drinks list
    getrennt separate
    gewähren to give
    gibt see geben
    glauben to think, to believe
    gleich shortly, immediately
        gleich hier vorne just here
das Gleis (-e) platform
das Golf golf
    groß big, large
die Größenordnung (-en) scale, amount
    Grüß Gott hallo
die Gulaschsuppe (-n) goulash soup
    gut good
        guten Appetit enjoy your meal

H

haben to have
    ich hatte I had
    ich hätte gern I'd like
die Haltestelle (-n) bus or tram stop
handeln: sich handeln um to refer to
der Handelsvertreter (-) agent (m.)
die Handelsvertreterin (-nen) agent (f.)
hat, hatte, hätte see haben
der Hauptausgang (¨-e) main exit
der Hauptbahnhof (¨-e) mainline station
der Hauptgang (¨-e) main course
das Hauptgericht (-e) main course
die Hauptgeschäftsstelle (-n) head office
das Haus (¨-er) house
    er/sie ist außer Haus he/she is not in
    Lieferung frei Haus carriage-free
die Haushaltswaren (pl.) household goods

das *Heilbuttsteak (-s)* halibut steak
die *Heimreise (-n)* journey home
heiß hot
helfen to help
der *Heringstopf (¨e)* pickled herring
der *Herr (-en)* gentleman
    Herr . . . Mr . . .
    Herr Ober! waiter
    Herr Wirt! landlord
herstellen (sep.) to produce
heute today
hier here
    gibt es hier . . . ? is there. . . .?
hierlassen (sep.) to leave here
die *Himbeertorte (-n)* raspberry flan
hin und zurück return (ticket)
hinterlassen to leave (a message)
holen to get, to fetch
hören to hear, to listen to
das *Hotel (-s)* hotel

I

ich I
ihn him, it
Ihnen you
Ihr, Ihre, Ihren, Ihrem, Ihrer your
immer always
    immer noch still
in in
innerhalb von within
interessieren: sich interessieren to be interested
    wir interessieren uns für we are interested in
irgendwelche, irgendwelcher any
ist see *sein*

J

ja yes
jawohl yes indeed
jetzt now

K

der *Kaffee (-s)* coffee
die *Kaffeemaschine (-n)* coffee machine
der *Kalbsbraten (-)* roast veal
kann see *können*
die *Karte (n)* menu, ticket
der *Katalog (-e)* catalogue
der *Kaufpreis (-e)* purchasing price
der *Kaufvertrag (¨e)* contract
    kein, keine, keinen, keinem, keiner no, not any
    keine Ahnung no idea
kennenlernen (sep.) to meet
der *Kilometer (-)* kilometre
der *Kiosk (-e)* kiosk
klären to settle
die *Klasse (-n)* class
    eine Fahrkarte zweiter Klasse a second-class ticket
klein small
der *Kloß (¨e)* dumpling
kommen to come, to get
können to be able to
    kann ich? can I?
    könnte ich? could I?
der *Kontakt (-e)* contact
das *Konto (Konten)* account
die *Kopie (-n)* copy
kosten to cost
die *Kraftbrühe (-n)* clear soup
die *Kreuzung (-en)* crossroads
der *Kunde (-n)* customer (m.)
die *Kundennummer (-n)* customer number

der Kundenrabatt (-e) customer discount
die Kundin (-nen) customer (f.)
kurz short, brief

L

die Lage (-n) position
das Lager (-) warehouse
    auf Lager in stock
der Lagerbestand (¨-e) stock
das Lammkotelett (-s) lamb chop
langsam slow(ly)
lassen see *zurücklassen*
laufen to run, to go
    wie läuft das Geschäft? how is business?
leicht easy
leid: es tut mir leid I'm sorry
leider unfortunately
die Leitung (-en) line (phone)
liebe(r) . . . dear . . .
der Lieferant (-en) supplier
die Lieferbedingungen (*pl.*) terms of delivery
die Liefermenge (-n) quantity delivered
der Lieferschein (-e) delivery paper
der Liefertermin (-e) delivery date
die Lieferung (-en) delivery
die Lieferzeit (-en) delivery time
die Linie (-n) number (tram or bus)
links left/on the left
lösen to solve (a problem)
die Luftpost air mail

M

machen to do
    das macht . . . DM that'll be . . . DM
die Mahngebühr (-en) fee for reminders
das Mal (-e) time
    das nächste Mal next time
mal see *einmal*
der Mangel (¨) fault
mangelfrei perfect
der Marktführer (-) market leader
der Marktanteil (-e) market share
die Maschine (-n) machine
mehr more
    mehr ist nicht drin that's the best I can do
mein, meine, meiner my
melden: sich melden to get in touch
die Menge (-n) quantity, amount
der Mengenrabatt (-e) discount for bulk purchase
das Menü (-s) set meal of the day
die Messe (-n) trade fair
mich me
der Mikrowellenherd (-e) microwave oven
die Minderung (-en) reduction
das Mineralwasser (-) mineral water
die Minute (-n) minute
mir (to) me
mit with
das Mittagessen (-) lunch
    zum Mittagessen einladen to invite to lunch
mitteilen (sep.) to inform
möchte see *mögen*
das Modell (-e) model
das Modem (-s) modem
mögen to like
    ich möchte I'd like to
möglich possible
der Moment (-e) moment
    Moment bitte one moment please

im Moment at the moment
- der Morgen (-) morning
  - *guten Morgen* good morning
- *morgen* tomorrow
- *müssen* to have to
- *MwSt. Schl.* short for *Mehrwertsteuer Schlüssel* VAT code

N

- *nach* to
- der Nachmittag (-e) afternoon
- die Nachricht (-en) message
  - *gute Nachrichten* good news
- *nachschauen* (sep.) to have a look
- die Nachspeise (-n) dessert
- *der, die, das nächste* the nearest, next
- die Nacht (¨-e) night
- der Nachtisch (-e) dessert
- die Nähe closeness
  - *in der Nähe* near/nearby
- der Name (-n) name
- *natürlich* of course
- *neben dem/der* next to the
- *nehmen* to take
- *nein* no
- *neu* new
- *nicht* not
- *noch mal* again
- die Nudelsuppe (-n) noodle soup
- die Nummer (-n) number

O

- *obenstehend* at the above (address)
- der Ober (-) waiter
  - *Ober!* waiter!
- das Obst (-) fruit
- der Obstsalat (-e) fruit salad
- *oder* or
- der Oktober October
- die Oper (-n) opera
- *Ordnung: in Ordnung* okay, fine

P

- *paar: ein paar* a few
- der Partner (-) partner (m.)
- die Party (-s) party
- der Passant (-en) passer-by (m.)
- die Passantin (-nen) passer-by (f.)
- *passen* to suit, to be suitable
- *per* by
  - *per Express* express delivery
- *persönlich* personal
- das Pils (-) pilsner (lager)
  - *ein kleines Pils* a small pilsner
- der Platz (¨-e) seat, place, space
  - *Platz nehmen* to take a seat
- die Pommes Frites (pl.) chips
- die Post (-) post office
- der Preis (-e) price
  - *zum Preis von* at (a price of)
- die Preisliste (-n) price list
- der Preisnachlaß (¨-e) price reduction
- *pro* per
- das Problem (-e) problem
- das Produkt (-e) product
- die Produktion (-en) production
- der Produktionsleiter (-) production manager (m.)
- die Produktionsleiterin (-nen) production manager (f.)
- die Produktionsschwierigkeiten (pl.) production problems
- die Produktpalette (-n) product range
- *produzieren* to produce

der Prospekt *(-e)* brochure
Prozent per cent

Q

die Qualität *(-en)* quality
die Quittung *(-en)* receipt

R

der Rabatt *(-e)* discount
die Rahmsauce *(-n)* cream sauce
rausgehen (sep.) to dispatch
die Rechnung *(-en)* invoice/bill
   eine Rechnung begleichen to settle an invoice
die Rechnungsnummer *(-n)* invoice number
recht: *recht haben* to be right
rechts right/on the right
reichhaltig substantial (meal)
der Reis *(-)* rice
die Reise *(-n)* journey
die Reklamation *(-en)* complaint
reservieren to reserve
der Rest *(-e)* rest
das Restaurant *(-s)* restaurant
die Rezeption *(-en)* reception
richtig correct
die Röstkartoffeln (pl.) fried potatoes
das Rotbarschfilet *(-s)* rosefish fillet
das Rotkraut (sing.) red cabbage
rückgängig machen to reverse, to cancel
der Ruhetag *(-e)* (lit.) rest day/closing day
das Rumpsteak *(-s)* rump steak
runter: hinunter down

S

die S-Bahn *(-en)* fast city train
der Sachbearbeiter *(-)* person responsible (m.)
die Sachertorte *(-n)* sachertorte, a rich chocolate cake
die Sahne *(-)* cream
der Salat *(-e)* salad
der Salat Niçoise salad niçoise
der Salatteller *(-)* mixed salad
die Salzkartoffeln (pl.) boiled potatoes
die Sauce *(-n)* sauce
der Sauerbraten *(-)* braised beef marinated in vinegar, herbs and raisins
schicken to send
die Schinkenplatte *(-n)* ham selection
schlecht bad
schmecken to taste (good)
   hat es Ihnen geschmeckt? did you enjoy the meal?
das Schnitzel *(-)* veal cutlet/schnitzel
schön nice, good
schreiben to write
das Schreiben *(-)* letter
schriftlich in writing
die Schwierigkeit *(-en)* difficulty
sehr very
   sehr gern I'd love to
   sehr geehrte(r) . . . dear . . .
sein to be
   ich bin I am
   er ist he is
die Seite *(-n)* page, side
   auf der linken Seite on the left-hand side
die Sekretärin *(-nen)* secretary (f.)
selbstverständlich certainly, of course

senden to send
sich oneself, yourself
sie they, she, it
Sie you (formal)
sieht aus see *aussehen*
das *Skonto (-s)* cash discount
so: so bald wie möglich as soon as possible
sofort immediately
spät late
später later
spätestens at the latest
die *Speisekarte (-n)* menu
sprechen to talk, to speak
stimmen to be correct
   das stimmt that's right
   stimmt so that's all right
die *Straße (-n)* street
die *Straßenbahn (-en)* tram
die *Stückzahl (-en)* number of items
suchen to look for, to seek

T

der *Tag (-e)* day
   guten Tag hallo
die *Tagesordnung (-en)* agenda
die *Tasche (-n)* bag
die *(Akten)tasche (-n)* briefcase
das *Taxi (-s)* taxi
der *Taxistand (¨e)* taxi rank
die *Taxizentrale (-n)* taxi centre
der *Tee (-s)* tea
die *Telefaxnachricht (-en)* fax message
das *Telefonat (-e)* phone conversation
das *Telefongespräch (-e)* call
die *Telefonnummer (-n)* phone number

der *Termin (-e)* date/appointment
teuer expensive
   wie teuer ist das? how much is it?
das *Theater (-)* theatre
trinken to drink
Tschüs! (col.) bye!
tun to do

U

die *U-Bahn (-en)* underground
die *U-Bahn Station* underground station
über about, over
überfällig overdue
überhitzen to overheat
übermitteln to transmit
die *Übernachtung (-en)* overnight stay
   pro Übernachtung per night
überprüfen to check
übersehen to overlook
überweisen to transfer (money)
um at
   um ... Uhr at ... o'clock
die *Unannehmlichkeit (-en)* inconvenience
und and
ungefähr about, roughly
uns (to) us
unser, unsere our
unsererseits on our part

V

das *Vanilleeis (-)* vanilla ice cream
verabschieden to say goodbye
veranlassen: bitte veranlassen please action
verbinden to put through (phone)

vereinbaren to agree, to arrange
   einen Termin vereinbaren to make an appointment
verkaufen to sell
der *Verkaufsleiter (-)* sales manager (m.)
die *Verkaufsleiterin (-nen)* sales manager (f.)
die *Verkaufsstelle (-n)* sales outlet
die *Verpackung (-en)* packaging
der *Versand (-)* dispatch (department)
die *Versandabteilung (-en)* dispatch department
die *Versandart (-en)* method of dispatch
   versandbereit ready for dispatch
die *Versicherung (-en)* insurance
das *Verständnis (-sse)* understanding
verstehen to understand
versuchen to try
der *Verteiler (-)* recipient
vertraulich confidential
der *Vertrieb (-)* distribution
verursachen to cause
die *Verzugszinsen* (pl.) interest on the overdue amount
viel a lot, much
   viel Spaß! have fun
   viele many
   vielen Dank many thanks
vielleicht perhaps
voll full
   voll belegt fully booked
vom short for *von dem*
von of, from
   von . . . bis from . . . to
vor dem/der in front of the
der *Vormittag (-e)* morning
vorrätig in stock
vorschlagen (sep.) to suggest
die *Vorspeise (-n)* starter
vorstellen (sep.) to introduce, to present

W

wählen to choose
wann when
die *Waren* (pl.) goods
warten to wait
warten auf to wait for
warum why
was what
die *Weinkarte (-n)* wine list
der *Wein (-e)* wine
weiß see *wissen*
weit far
   wie weit? how far?
welcher? welche? welches? what? which?
wenig little
wie? how?
wieder again
wiederholen to repeat
Wiederhören: auf Wiederhören! goodbye! (phone)
Wiedersehen: auf Wiedersehen goodbye
wieviel? how much
wir we
wirklich real, really
wissen to know
   ich weiß nicht I don't know
wo where
die *Woche (-n)* week
das *Wochenende (-n)* weekend
wollen to wish, to want
würden (Sie . . . ?) would (you . . . ?)
   ich würde gern(e) . . . I'd like to . . .

Z

zahlen to pay
   wir möchten zahlen, bitte we'd like the bill, please
die *Zahlung (-en)* payment
die *Zahlungsaufforderung (-en)* request for payment
die *Zahlungsbedingungen (pl.)* payment terms
das *Zeichen (-)* sign
   unser/Ihr Zeichen our/your reference
die *Zeit (-en)* time
   für diese Zeit on these days
die *Zentrale (-n)* switchboard
das *Zimmer (-)* room
die *Zimmerreservierung (-en)* room reservation
die *Zone (-n)* zone
der *Zug (¨-e)* train
der *Zulieferer (-)* supplier
zum: zu dem to the
   zum 1. Dez. for 1 Dec.
zunächst first (of all)
   zunächst einmal first of all
zur: zu der to the
zurück back
zurücklassen (sep.) to leave (behind)
zurückrufen (sep.) to call back
zusammen together
die *Zusammenarbeit (sing.)* cooperation
zusammenarbeiten (sep.) to cooperate, to work together
zweite, zweiter second
zweitens secondly
die *Zwiebelsuppe (-n)* onion soup